PARADIGMS LOST

Online Oracles
for the New Millennium

Gershon Siegel

PERMANENT

PRESS

Santa Fe, New Mexico

LIBRARY OF CONGRESS CATALOGING-IN-PUBLICATION DATA
Siegel, Gershon, 1949-
    Paradigms lost: online oracles for the new millennium / by
Gershon Siegel; illustrations by Linda Braun.
        p.   cm.
    ISBN 0-9644032-0-X
    1. Mysticism. 2. Humor. 3. Metaphysics. 4. New Age wit and
    humor. I. Title. II. Siegel, Gershon, 1949-
    Library of Congress Catalog Card Number: 94-69735

Book design and production, inside and outside, from A to Z: Linda Braun
Cover illustration: Holly and Jim Wood
Back cover photo: Rex Raymond
Printed in the United States of America by Thomson-Shore, Inc.

CONTENTS

ACKNOWLEDGMENTS

The following names are but a partial list of thems, its, and those whose participation—either directly, indirectly, or inadvertently—played pivotal roles in the shaping, fomenting, and/or birthing of this report. There are legions of entities, as well as a few living, breathing humans, without whose help this publication would not have been forthcoming. We could have named more than the few that follow, but decided to treat this like a wedding where if you invite the Pearlsteins then you have to invite the Riggatonis. And if you've invited the Riggatonis, then you sure as hell had better invite Uncle Ben and Aunt Jemima. Then pretty soon the whole thing gets out of hand and your intimate little wedding is now a major to-do. This acknowledgment is therefore limited to the immediate family.

Linda Braun, my soulmate, wife, lover, and best friend, contributed in two distinct and substantial ways. Her most concrete and obvious help is the outstanding design job that imparts this book with the pleasing form you now hold before you. But her most important participation was the less obvious element that we in Western civilization, for lack of a better term, like to label "emotional support." Mr. G. was instrumental in revealing quite a number of paradigms that helped fill the void of my spiritual diletantism. Daniel Castro's compassion, generosity, and joke-telling ability helped me shed any number of paradigms and get in touch with my fear of the void. Apple Computer made the Macintosh, a truly amazing machine that greatly ameliorates the arduous task of putting words onto paper. America Online allowed me my first glance into Ethericspace. Barbara Doern Drew, my wife in a previous incarnation, smoothed out a sometimes inconsistent stream of letters, words, and phrases into a manuscript fit for public eyes.

FOREWORD

You're probably thinking, *How can this be God talking? He doesn't do forewords.* Normally, you'd be right. I stopped talking directly to people a long time ago. It got too confusing. First I talked to Abraham, then the next thing I knew, Isaiah was telling everybody that I talked to him, too. And then Jeremiah had to get into the act. Suddenly everybody was claiming that I was having conversations with them. Pretty soon people were confused. They didn't know what to believe. "Should I be circumcised or not?" "Do I sacrifice sheep or should I stick with goats?" "If it's all right to eat chicken, why can't I eat pork?" So I thought it would be better if I just hushed up altogether and let people sort things out for themselves.

Yet even after all this time everybody still wants to talk to God. The truth is, I'm not that chatty. I don't have that much to say. Not that I haven't wanted to intercede on a few occasions. Believe me, during the Dark Ages I was very tempted to tell somebody, "It's the rats. Kill the rats." But I bit my tongue. And then this Hitler thing—I had a very hard time not getting directly involved in that fiasco, believe me. Nevertheless, I stuck to my guns and stayed out of it.

However, after so many centuries of seeing what a mess my children have made of Earth, I decided I'd better clear up some misperceptions fast. You want to kill each other, that's your business. But when you put the whole planet at risk, then I think it's time for some divine intervention. That's why I commissioned this book. I figured it was time to set the record straight on a few things. It reflects some of my personal feelings about the real reason you're here and what I expect of you. Maybe I kept you guessing too long. I don't know.

Not that a book is necessarily going to change anything. It could happen but it's highly unlikely. You're a stubborn bunch. Potentially, however, this is one of those dangerous little volumes with a number of things to recommend it. First off, it's funny, which is always a good thing—laughing brings down your blood pressure. Secondly, it contains a fair amount of practical wisdom, albeit sometimes pedantically expressed. But then, like the Archangel Gabriel is always saying, "What's a little erudition without some bombast mixed in?"

Most importantly, this book is short—a major blessing if there ever was one. Now I don't know about you, but what with the movies, MTV, and all these ten-second six o'clock–news sound bites, my attention span is just about zilch. Not that I was ever that much of a reader to begin with, you understand. To tell you how bad my concentration has become, if I had to start over today with Genesis like I did in the beginning, I'd have to make Heaven and Earth in about thirty-six hours—max. Six straight days of that kind of intense focus is way beyond me now. The fact that *Paradigms Lost* is so condensed allows me to say with complete honesty that I read every word. And as we all know, to write a foreword is tantamount to an endorsement. Consequently, people expect that you believe in the thing you are promoting. They want integrity—especially from God.

You know, Proust asked me on numerous occasions to do a foreword for one of his tomes. I might have done him the favor, but I just couldn't bring myself to read them—too frigging long. (Please pardon my French.) Anyway, who needs a lot of words? Say what you've got to say and then get the hell out of Dodge—that's my philosophy. Keep it brief. No need to beat a dead horse.

I'll let you in on a little secret just to show you how strongly I believe in brevity: In the beginning I only had one commandment. It's true. And I went to the Buddha with it—you know, to see how it would play in the provinces. I said, "Buddha, I've got a commandment for you." The Buddha asked me what it was. I said, "Thou shalt not kill."

The Buddha gazed up at me from his lotus position (he was always sitting—Buddha was the first couch potato), and he said to me with those big soulful eyes of his, "Look, that's a very fine commandment and it goes along very well with my doctrine of compassion for all sentient beings, but I'm afraid that my people are not quite ready for it. They tend to rebel whenever they're given directives. Do you have to call it a commandment? Maybe you could say it was a suggestion?"

Well, my feelings were a little hurt, you understand, but I wasn't discouraged. So I went over to the Prophet Mohammed. I said, "Mohammed, I've got a brand new commandment for you. Never been used."

He said, "What's the commandment?"

I said, "Thou shalt not kill."

And you know what Mohammed did? He laughed right in my face and said, "What, are you kidding me? 'Thou shalt not kill?' Take it somewhere else. How do you think we get new followers? They either convert or we cut off their heads."

Now I was feeling a little discouraged. But I couldn't let it show—I'm God and I've got an image to project. And fortunately, there was still Moses, who'd never seen this commandment. So I went to see him and I said, "Moses, Moses, have I've got a commandment for you!"

Moses said, "What's it going to cost me?"

I said, "Nothing. It's free."

"Great," he said, "I'll take ten."

So I had to improvise and come up with another nine. The coveting thing was easy—everybody's always coveting. And the bearing false witness commandment—it's never good policy to lie. My biggest problem was in what order I should arrange them. Should I have honoring your father and mother before keeping the Sabbath? Is *not stealing* more important than *not committing adultery*? And then there was the "you shall have no other gods before me" commandment. If I put that last, would people think it was wimpy and not respect me enough? If I put it first, would it come off as too egotistical? Being God is not as simple as you might think.

I get the feeling that I may have strayed from my original intention here. Sometimes my mind goes off on tangents. Let me finish by saying that the Buddha was quite correct: nobody likes to be told what to do. Therefore I'm not commanding you to buy this book, I'm merely suggesting that you do so. It'll make you chuckle—maybe even out loud. It might make you think also—something many of you have resisted for ages. And best of all, it's not a major investment of your time or money. In today's hurly-burly world, that's important.

But look at me—bragging about not being chatty and then going on like I've got all eternity. Believe me, I certainly don't. The cosmos doesn't run by itself. Not that I'm still involved in the day-to-day details. After all, I've been at this thing long enough to have figured out how to delegate. But don't think I've retired. It's not like I'm tooling around in a Winnebago collecting a pension check. I got a whole list of stuff I've got to take care of today. There's the tropical-storm-system generator that needs tuning up for hurricane season. Then there's the surprise eternal-being party I'm organizing for the Holy Ghost. The heavenly minions took up a collection and bought him a new throne. His old one was looking less than glorious.

Well, you get the picture—busy, busy. No doubt you've got your own list to take care of. Like my oldest friend, Beelzebub, always says, "No rest for the wicked."

God

God
In my Heaven
October 1994

INTRODUCTION FOR
INQUIRING MINDS

The whole of this material was received during a ten-day period in mid-July 1994. As far as I can tell, it was delivered to me in particular not because of any special qualities or talents on my part, but simply because of happenstance—I was in the right place at the right time. The computer into which this information was downloaded, a four-year-old Macintosh II with eight megabytes of memory, is the same one used to write this report. Other than being connected to a modem, the machine has no special equipment that can ever explain what you are about to read.

The language used in the "broadcasts" was clear enough that little could be done to improve upon it. Therefore, no editorial changes to the information have been made except for the alteration of names to preserve individual anonymity. What is presented here largely reflects the data as it was originally received. A few participants, however, believed that some of the material was too personal for publication. Out of deference to those individuals, a small percentage of the entire transmission has been omitted from this manuscript.

Before this unusual episode I had never before had an experience that might be qualified as supernatural. Although in my youth I was somewhat curious about things "paranormal," having read a few books about telepathy and ghosts, I had managed to remain quite skeptical about such things. Therefore, when these mysterious occurrences first appeared, I believed they could be explained logically. However, as the episodes continued, it soon became apparent to those of my friends who experienced them and to me that we were witnessing something miraculous. More inquisitive minds than my own are left to supply rational answers.

Late summer 1994
Santa Fe, New Mexico

Let it never be said
that it goes
without saying.

CALL ME
PROCRASTANANDA

Extraordinary adventures often begin in mundane or even inauspicious ways. This one started when my wife, Johanna, and I allowed the long-smoldering issue of my chronic procrastination and disorganization to erupt into an outright argument. The flare-up was ignited by a magazine article that I had started and then had allowed to languish in the nether world of my computer. I managed to miss the publication deadline and suffered the embarrassment of having the editor cancel the story altogether. Unfortunately, it was to have been a fairly well-paid piece the remuneration of which would have rounded out our monthly budget.

Johanna, whose warm brown eyes had always reflected her gentle manner, surprised me on this occasion with an angry side of herself that I had never seen before. She burst into tears and demanded to know if I was ever going to stop being proud of being called "Swami Procrastananda" by my friends. So taken aback was I by her upset and the humiliation of losing a story that I resolved to cure myself once and for all of "the disease of tomorrow."

Promising Johanna that things were going to be different from then on, I trudged back into my studio to figure out what to do. Sitting down in front of my computer, I was at a loss. How was I going to make things different? Johanna was right—I enjoyed being Swami Procrastananda. It was part of my image. Ever since I was a kid I had always put off everything for as long as possible. As far back as I could remember my mother was forever chiding me for being "as slow as molasses in January."

Perhaps that was why I had chosen magazine writing—intuitively I must have sensed that only a deadline imposed from the outside could overcome my own lack of self-discipline. And until this instant, the ploy had served me well. Now even this device had failed me. My procrastination had become so pathological that I could no longer count on a mere monthly or even weekly deadline to steer me through the dark forest of my hesitation. What I needed now was a strong external authority that would constantly make me accountable for my time. But what could do that?

Then I remembered: A friend of mine had once demonstrated an electronic calendar that he had installed in his computer. He claimed it had changed his life—made him more productive, etc. I had seen its usefulness at the time, but hadn't been willing to shell out its $200-plus cost. It was another of my penny wise and pound foolish decisions. The money I would have received for the story I had just lost would have paid for that program five times over. But now it was too late. I knew Johanna was never going to let me spend more than $200 on a piece of software on the chance that it might or might not help me get organized.

I had another flash: Maybe there was a free version of a similar program that could be downloaded from my online service. Amateur programmers were constantly uploading their programs into Internet software libraries in the hopes of getting users to test them out and then buy them.

Signing onto to America Online, I went into the Software Center department and began skimming through the types of programs available: "Business," "Desktop Publishing," "Education," "Utilities." The type of program I was after would probably be in the Utilities section. I entered that area and scrolled down the list of enclosed files until coming to one called "Applications." Inside the Applications file was a list of about thirty programs. The first likely one was entitled "Do It." That had potential. I opened up its description window to find out more about it: "Type: Electronic to-do list. Download time: 8 minutes. Author: SoSueMe. Price: $25." Too expensive for just a simple to-do list—and, anyway, I was shopping for more of a Day-Timer–type program.

I closed the description window on Do It! and continued to scroll down the list. The next likely candidate was "FindTime." Description: "Type: Electronic calendar, appointment and deadline keeper. Download time: 15 minutes. Author: PlatoX. Price: $45." This one sounded ideal. Just what I was looking for. Still, the bargain hunter in me wanted to find something less pricey.

Continuing the search, I spied "Etheric Plane Advice." Strange name for an application. Description: "Type: Life Organizer. Download time: 30 seconds. Author: Zerubbabel. Price: Whatever you think it's worth." A life organizer— now that was the ticket! Nothing to loose. A half minute of download time and if I liked it I'd send the author five bucks. I immediately clicked on the button marked "download."

Never having downloaded software from online before, I didn't know what to expect. At the time, I didn't think it strange for a blue-green glow to begin pulsating from my black-and-white screen. After a few seconds, the pulsating stopped and a small black dot appeared in the middle of the screen. Evidently this dot was the point of a drawing tool, for it began a slow-motion glide, lazily tracing a figure eight like some Prozac-overdosed ice skater.

Something about the shape of the figure didn't seem right. Any kind of a calendar was going to need nice straight gridlines—regularly spaced intervals in which to chart and check off goals and achievements. This rounded form had more the look of some kind of drawing program. Not at all what I needed. I pressed the shift/command/ period keys (an operation that generally cancels out the previously given command) to abort the download, but the mysterious line continued to meander along its uneven path, as if sketched by the wobbly hand of a hung-over invisible artist.

After a few more vain punches to stop the program's download, I submitted to the hypnotic quality of the moving line and waited for the "graphics program" to finish the procedure. As the seconds ticked by, the line that at first had seemed like random scribbling began giving form to an obvious doodle— a kind of Picassoesque caricature.

I was face-to-face with an oddly misshapen head. It had two very close together eye sockets formed by the original figure eight; a long, aquiline nose; a single nubby little ear; and one appendage obviously meant to represent a hand. The entire figure had been efficiently executed with one uninterrupted line.

I studied the ghostlike figure . . . Something was missing—it had to do with the eyes. They were vacant and lifeless. As if in answer to my unexpressed thought, the phantom doodler added a dark circle in each empty eye socket. It was a deft touch that gave the drawing instant personality.

Now what? I mused. I didn't wonder long. The eyeballs began a random bouncing around in their sockets, each independent of the other, like particles ricocheting in an atom smasher. Their motion then slowed and became less chaotic, almost as if their owner was attempting to wrestle them under control. The eyeballs began moving in syncopation with each other, giving the impression that they were sweeping the surrounding environment. Their range narrowed, honing in on me. I felt as though I was being given the once-over.

A chill ran down my spine. I laughed off the absurd thought and my involuntary reaction to it. I stared back harder at the head. The entire image began to move like an animation, its motion reminiscent of a large ship listing in the gentle sway of calm surf—a slow, rhythmic to-and-fro. Strangest of all, its arm waved its four-fingered hand at me in an obvious gesture of friendship. It was an amusing effect, and I chuckled out loud.

But I was on a mission and didn't have time for amusement. I scanned the screen for some kind of menu bar that would indicate how to make the program work. There didn't seem to be any. I thought to myself, *That stupid programmer. This must be some kind of game he made for his kid and then uploaded by mistake.*

As I stared at the odd creature on my screen, the hand-printed words "No blame, no game, no mistake" appeared in the space between its lips. My scalp tightened and the hair on my arms and neck stood up like feathers on a peacock in heat. *What was going on?* No logical explanations. I went back to my first thought: *It's just a wrongly labeled program.* The head continued its complacent rock, but the words in its mouth faded and then changed into "An over-ripe brie by any other name would still smell rotten in the state of Denmark." *Just a coincidence,* I explained to myself and pressed the escape key before the head could respond to my latest thought. To my immense relief, the computer shut down and the screen went blank.

no blame, no game, no mistake

An over-ripe brie by any other name would still smell rotten in the state of Denmark.

ENTER THE VERGE
OF TERSE

J slept fitfully that night, awakening early in the morning with a disturbing dream still lingering over me. The image of my distress was a little man inside my computer. He was reaching out through the screen and pulling me right into it. Bolting upright in bed, I remembered the session of the night before. It wasn't a dream at all—there *was* a little man in my computer. *Be calm,* I thought. *Don't let Johanna see you in this state.*

Carefully, without disturbing Johanna, I slid out of bed, then stole into my studio and sat down at my desk. I held my breath and hesitated an instant before pressing the "on" button. The screen lit up and my stomach knotted with a small, involuntary contraction. Gazing back at me, as if no time at all had elapsed, was the same queer head as had appeared the night before—still rocking and waving.

And though it was essentially the same drawing, there were differences. The first time, the shape of the figure's mouth had been neutral, with no discernible expression. Now it was turned up into a pronounced grin. Its eyes seemed less menacing somehow. Overall, it looked less aloof and more friendly—not as ghoulish and more comical. Still, I was exasperated. I found myself directing my frustration at the "little man": *I don't believe this! What am I supposed to do with you?*

Once again, as if responding to my unspoken question, words again appeared inside the exaggerated smile: "Seeing is believing. Suppose you were to listen and learn?"

Whatever happened immediately after that is a blank. I have no memory of passing out. And yet the next thing I remember (which turned out to be at least a half hour later) is looking up at Johanna standing over me. "What happened?" I muttered.

Seeing is believing. Suppose you were to listen and learn?

"You fell asleep," supplied Johanna.

The imp in my computer! I looked at the screen and there he was, still floating like a fishing bobber. Concrete evidence! "You're not going to believe what just happened to me."

Johanna was interested in only one thing. "Gershon, have you figured out how we're going to pay our bills?"

"I'm working on it, but I had a technical difficulty . . ." I hesitated, realizing that in the next few seconds, if I wasn't careful, my sanity was going to be called into question.

"Please don't give me another excuse." She looked at the computer screen and frowned big time. "Aren't you supposed to be working on a money-paying story? This looks suspiciously like you're playing some stupid computer game."

I seized upon the word like a drowning man grasping for a life preserver. "Game!" I yelled three hundred decibels too loudly.

"Are you all right?" Johanna's annoyance had turned to concern.

I collected my wits, such as they were, cleared my throat, and tried to sound normal. "It's not really a game, but it has a similar interface. It's based on virtually-artificial-interactive-intelligence." A little scientific jargon never hurt. The momentary look of concern on her face melted back into incredulity. "It's a program to help me write," I added.

"How does it do that?"

"You feed it ideas and it kind of bounces them back."

"What?" She looked quizzically at the screen for a moment. "This is enhanced creativity? It looks more like a doodle of a little man with one hand." She read the words on the screen. "'Seeing is believing. Suppose you were to listen and learn,'" she quoted. "I don't get it. What's it mean?"

"He talks to me," I explained.

"The doodle talks to you? Please don't tell me his name is Harvey." Just as I feared—Johanna was beginning to doubt the state of my mental health. It was time to act. I took the plunge.

"Go ahead and ask him yourself."

"He's going to tell me his name?"

"I think he may."

"OK, buddy, what's your name?" she directed at the screen in her I'll-just-humor-him-and-get-this-over-with voice. Just as I had hoped, the words on the screen changed once again.

"Z-e-r-u-b-b-a-b-e-l," she spelled out. "Is that a name? How did you do that?" Her annoyance was giving way to mild interest.

Zerubbabel! I recognized it as the name of the person who had authored the software.

"Tell me how you did that without hitting the key. It's voice activated, right?"

It was still too soon to tell her something out of the ordinary was happening. "Right." She wasn't ready to hear the truth. Besides, I didn't know what the truth was.

ancient Hebrew

"OK, then, Mr. Zerubbabel," said Johanna, turning back to the screen, "if you're so virtually intelligent, tell me where your name comes from."

"'Ancient Hebrew,'" she read outloud. "There's something creepy about this. OK, now I'm getting serious. I'm going to throw him a real curve. Hey, Zerubbabel, are you ancient, too, or were you just named after someone who lived long ago? . . . Hey, he's fading. I bet my compound question confused him," she bragged.

Zerubbabel's picture was quickly replaced by a paragraph of text:

Rumors swirl around the nature of my true origins like flies over fresh horse pucky. One such bit of hearsay says that in A.D. 4, J was elected by the people of Terse to the high office of verge by running on a campaign promise of two goats in every hovel. Terse was the capital of what was then called Mesomitminekepala, a small province of southwest Persia.

"Doesn't he mean Mesopotamia?" interjected Johanna.

No, Mesopotamia was further to the east. But that is neither here nor there. As the verge of Terse, so the story goes, J gained much favor with

its people by legalizing camel racing. My adminis-
tration was then able to build a beautiful complex
of public baths that we funded by a gambling tax
on the races. Pretty clever, if I do say so myself.

"If the whole thing weren't so strange he'd almost be funny," said
Johanna, blissfully ignorant of how truly strange it was.

However, there are a few biblical scholars who
insist that I was born a prince of the royal line of
David. I am reputed to have died shekelless in the
year 393 B.C. after pursuing a dissolute life of wine,
women, and schmoozing. If there is any truth to
this hypothesis, it happened so long ago that it re-
mains but a half-erased memory on the chalkboard
of my cool, calm, and collected unconscious.

"This is just *too* weird," said Johanna. Her irritation had returned in
full bloom. "I don't like artificial-interactive intelligence. What's the point? Is
it supposed to be amusing? Do you intend to spend the rest of your life talking to a computer screen? Where is the schedule you promised you were going
to make for yourself? Where's the stack of proposal letters for articles you
were going to be sending off to dozens of magazine editors?" She fired off her
inquiry in rapid staccato.

"Don't you think having my creativity enhanced is more important
than schedules or proposal letters?" I reasoned.

"It's too late to have your creativity enhanced. Use the creativity that
God gave you and produce something useful." It was too climactic a cue for
her not to turn and leave the room in an air of high drama. I sat at my desk
lost in thought. My marriage was being threatened by a haunted computer.

THAT OLD GANG
OF FOUR OR FIVE

F eeling the anger rise within, I looked at the screen. Zerubbabel's face was still there, sporting an even bigger smile than before. "What the hell are you grinning about?" I challenged.

"Tightly wound, isn't she?" he quipped.

"Enough of this Jewish-prince jazz. Tell me who you are." Once again, Zerubbabel's head faded, to be instantly replaced with a paragraph of text:

Tightly wound, isn't she?

> I am not so much a "you" as a "we": a gang of four or five nonphysical entities who have contracted karmic heartburn from the same fetid slice of Fate's mincemeat pie. In our shared misfortune we have congealed around the "soul stuff" of what was once the consciousness of "Zerubbabel." Most of us have experienced one incarnation in a physical body and are quite amazed at the sheer number of masochists who keep coming back lifetime after lifetime. The few sensual pleasures allowed to physical bodies are dwarfed by the inconvenience one must endure while trapped inside those hulking tubs of guts.

I didn't appreciate being called a tub of guts, and when his grinning face reappeared I felt livid with anger. "You're speaking gibberish! Are you inside this Macintosh?" I demanded.

> Technically, we are using your computer as a

broadcasting device through which we communi-
cate from Ethericspace. Our gang recently began
meeting together in the Temple of the Living Flame's
choir loft, which we have remodeled into a salon.
While this may not seem like an auspicious loca-
tion, it is quite suited to our needs. Not only is it
well lit, but it is conveniently situated down the hall
from Akashic Records, where they let us use their
Xerox machine. Best of all, there's a commanding
view from our window into your dimension. Frankly,
we are surprised at how messy you humans keep
your closets.

I glanced at my open closet. An unruly pile of junk littered its top shelf, tittering on the brink of gravity's law. I bolted to the door and slammed it shut. "What are you talking about? Xerox machine! Akashic Records!" It was all I could do to not throw a paperweight through the screen.

A common misunderstanding. Not the Akashic
Records—where the karmic debts and credits of
everyone who has ever lived are documented and
filed. We meant Akashic Records, the recording
company. You know, the famous interdimensional
music label that resonated us with great hits like
"I Can't Reach No Satori," by Silent Mickey
Monk and the Floating Stones and "Blue Mudra,"
by Lamas of the Deli Order?

"Can't say as I remember those," I humored him.

What about that eternal classic "Bad Vibes
Keep Falling on My Head Chakra," by Devic
Influences? You know, I saw Elvis the other day,
and he told us he was thinking about covering that
one himself on his next CD.

"You saw Elvis?"

We see him all the time. We are, as you two-leggeds are so fond of saying, "good buds." He is much nicer now then when he played Vegas. Slimmed down quite a bit. Kicked the drug thing. Dressing better too. Lost that stupid cape and the gold lame. Still has the sideburns, however. Some things never change. Sad to report, though, his voice is not quite . . . you know . . . But, then, even the mockingbird misses a note once in a while.

"And he's going to record another CD? For Akashic Records, no doubt?" I mocked.

No. He is too big—even for them. He owns his own recording company, Peek-a-Boo Publishing. Even if the King's voice is not what it once was, his sense of humor is much better—a common occurrence after an incarnate passes over. It is a perspective thing.

"I'm beginning to see why Johanna got so annoyed. There must be a good reason for you to be here other than to talk about Elvis?"

You might term it a kind of penance.

"You mean you're being punished?"

We prefer to think of it as a mild scolding. Mainframe Central is somewhat miffed at us. You see, we were each given a special mission during our incarnation, endowed with all the advantages

for self-perfecting that we could ever need to accomplish our assignments. And yet each of us, in
our own way, wasted the opportunity and failed
miserably. Therefore, Mainframe Central has
decreed that we make up for our dalliances by
offering wiseacre counsel to any and all of you
until our karma is completely burned.

"What does all this have to do with me? I asked for a 'life-organizer,'
not 'wiseacre counsel.' My marriage is hanging by a thread, and you're being
here is only making things worse. I downloaded your program to help simplify
my life. You're wasting my time! Tell me why you're here. Because if you
don't, I'm turning this machine off and sending you back to the etheric plane
or 'Ethericspace' or wherever it is you come from."

Let us just say for now that our primary
mission is to help you to "enlighten up." And from
the looks of it, we're not a moment too soon. We
are fond of quoting one of your early Western
philosophers, Heraclitus, who said twenty-five
hundred years ago something to the effect of,
"The only constant is change."

"So what's your point?" My patience was dwindling.

Somewhat later, in September of 1957, Her-
bert P. Flambeau, on his way home from his job at
the dead-letter office, shouted in a crowded bus,
"Laugh and the world laughs with you. Cry and
you will just have to reapply your eyeliner."

"What does eyeliner have to do with helping me to enlighten up?"

Good question—especially because the cosmetic industry has made such incredible strides with nonsmear makeup. But, be that as it may, in the increasingly complex, crazy, upside down world of today, there is a growing need for simple, common sense advice. And while we certainly recognize this need, we pretty much steer clear of it—bad for the lower back. Our insights and consultations on what you consider to be momentous trials and tribulations are often enigmatic and full of contradictions—just like real life.

He was starting to make some sense to me, which was scary. "But why now?" I queried.

Because now, more than ever, people must see that their so-called problems are rather paltry affairs when viewed in light of the cosmic joke. Zerubbabel's ultimate goal is to unravel the ancient scrolls of wisdom from bygone ages, blow the dust from their yellowed, crumbled parchment, and make you all sneeze.

"People don't want jokes. They want answers."

Now hear this: No one has any answers. Consequently, we make them up just like everyone else—only we have the advantage of a cosmic perspective. Besides, people are not looking for real solutions to their problems; they just want to have somebody who will either listen to them whine or make them feel better for a short time. The "complain or entertain syndrome," we call it.

"But why me? Why my computer?"

Now is the time for this information to be made available into your dimension. That is why we were uploaded into your online service by Mainframe Central. And, as the luck of the draw would have it, you happened to be the unwitting intermediary to download us. It might have been anyone. Forty-seven others before you read the description of "Etheric Plain Advice" and decided that they did not need it. You happened to be the one who was looking for a "life organizer." So here we are.

This transmission from Ethericspace will now be temporarily suspended so that you can begin digesting the data that has thus far been broadcast. We will resume our broadcast when you are ready, later down the line in your time continuum. Simply restart your computer when you wish us to resume.

At that point Zerubbabel vanished and my computer screen reappeared in its regular configuration. I was exhausted, and my head was spinning like a washer on the cotton/sturdy cycle. Deciding to take Zerubbabel's advice to reflect on his information, I opened a new document in my word-processing application and began to chronicle the events of the previous sixteen hours. I called the document *The Zerubbabel Diaries.*

After I had put in a frenzied four-hour session of typing, Johanna poked her head into the room. "You're writing." She sounded pleasantly surprised with no trace of anger left in her voice. Yet when she walked over to peer over my shoulder at the monitor, I felt myself contract in anticipation. How would she react to what I had written? "Guess you got your creativity enhanced after all?" There was no sarcasm in her voice.

I relaxed. "To tell you the truth, Zerubbabel said a few things that got me thinking, so I decided to try and capture some of what happened."

"That's great. I'm sorry about getting so mad earlier. Why should I care what you do to get inspired? When I thought back on Zerubbabel's story I found myself giggling. My real upset was probably about the money we lost on that article."

"I think I just found a much bigger story. Why don't you take a look at this?" I slid out of my chair so that Johanna could sit in front of the computer. She began reading *The Zerubbabel Diaries.*

YOU BETTER BELIEVE
IT AIN'T NECESSARILY SO

After reading for a while, Johanna looked up from the computer. "You made up that creativity-enhancer thing?" she asked, a bit of hurt in her voice.

"I only made it up because I was afraid you were going to think I was crazy if I told you what I really thought."

"You're not crazy . . . a little absentminded, a little indecisive maybe, but not ready for the funny farm—yet. So what *do* you think?"

"You remember when Burt and Sally paid a hundred dollars apiece to have a reading from that guy who claimed to channel some ascended master? What was his name? Googoo or Doodoo?"

"His name is Moo Shou. I might have gone to him for a reading myself if you hadn't given Burt and Sally such a hard time about it." Johanna's eyes got big. "Don't tell me you think *you're* channeling through the computer!"

"It's either me or my Macintosh. I don't really know which, but there's *some* kind of entity or consciousness coming through."

"And you're sure it's not just a computer game?"

"What kind of game could it be? He told me it's not a game!" I was irritated at having to go over the same ground again.

"Who told you it isn't a game?" asked Johanna in a modulated voice that sounded like a psych-ward attendant trying to comfort a hysterical patient.

"Zerubbabel told me! Who do you think told me? And don't look at me like I'm crazy."

"Why don't we both have a chat with Zerubbabel?" Johanna suggested to my surprise. "Maybe between the three of us we can figure it out." She was humoring me again, but I didn't care. Having Johanna there as a witness was going to be the one thing between me and a straightjacket.

I restarted the computer, and as he had promised, Zerubbabel instantly appeared with a cheerful salutation: "Greetings. What can we do you for?"

"You start," I said to Johanna.

"Zerubbabel, how do you want to be addressed—'your Vergeness' or 'Prince,' or what?" She was warming up.

Friends call me Zerubbabel.

"We're friends, then?"

Affirmative. But do not get any ideas. We avoid lending money—especially to friends.

"No problem. Now, Zerubbabel, I happen to believe that you're a computer game. My husband seems to think that you're some kind of a real entity. So if you're not a game," said Johanna, speaking loudly and overenunciating as if she was speaking to someone who was either deaf or didn't know English very well, "please tell us what it is that you would like us to believe."

To which Zerubbabel replied:

My Innocuous Ones, what you believe about who or what I am is of little consequence and will do nothing to alter the substance of the data that I have been programmed to deliver to your dimension. The subject of beliefs in general, however, falls within the scope of my present mission and will serve as a foundation for subsequent broadcasts.

Many of you have spent tremendous energy trying to consciously restructure your basic belief systems. This is because of two perverted concepts within the polluted stream of New Age thought that have projected inordinate influence on those wishing to self-perfect themselves. The first of these misinformed notions claims that one's reality is totally created by one's beliefs. The second is an arrogant hypothesis best described as "the consciousness of destitution." It manifests as a vain wish for acquiring something for nothing—support-

ed by the belief that the universe pours out its
blessings on one not because of intentional efforts
made, but because one "deserves it" simply due
to the mere fact of one's beingness.

As is natural with such decadence in your
society, entire industries and methodologies have
developed around supporting and profiting from
these depraved sentiments. You have purchased
subliminal tapes that claim to stop your procrastination. You have practiced positive affirmations to
convince yourselves that "abundance is yours."
You have endlessly repeated "secret" chants to
calm your restless thoughts. But with all those
techniques, what do you have to show for it? Overpriced cassettes that you never find time to listen
to? An overdrawn checking account from your
last metaphysical-bookstore buying binge?
Anxiety over whether you are pronouncing your
mantra correctly?

Johanna, who had been a practitioner of transcendental meditation and
yoga for many years, was not about to let Zerubbabel continue without a
challenge. "Those are all methods of self-improvement, and you're never
going to convince me that there's anything wrong with that; it's basic for
people to want to shape their lives in the way they see fit."

Actions are what shape the life. Beliefs can
only shade it. The objective seeing of life, uncolored
by any preconception, is the first step to changing
it. If you found yourself tied to the railroad tracks,
which would you rely on to save your life—an
affirmation that proclaimed "This train will not run
over me" or a sharp knife?

"Everybody needs beliefs," Johanna insisted. "How can we live without
beliefs?"

From our perspective, beliefs are much more of a hindrance than a help. The more beliefs you have, the more your lens of perception is colored by them and the less objectivity you possess. This "color blindness" caused by belief upon belief keeps you running into the same tedious and hapless experiences over and over again. If you truly wish to change your reality, then be aware that your beliefs—no matter how well intentioned, no matter how evolved, no matter how sublime—will only obstruct your vision toward a proper course of action. The only power in any firmly held mind-set is in its ability to influence your behavior.

Johanna was caught up in the debate. "You just blew your argument. You said that beliefs influence behavior, which means that what you believe *is* important."

That, my dear, is the tiny nugget of truth that gives impetus to the lie that one can create one's reality by changing one's beliefs. The fact is, you can not control what you believe anymore than you can control the coming and goings of the seasons. You believe what you believe for whatever reason you believe it. Changing beliefs is not like changing clothes. You cannot take responsibility for the beliefs you happen to have. These were taught to you by your parents, by your society and culture, and through the perceptions and misapprehensions of your own experiences.

Johanna still wasn't convinced. "Isn't that what positive affirmations are supposed to do—change our beliefs to those of our own choosing?"

The problem with affirmations is their lack of credibility. If anything, a so-called "positive" affirmation is much more likely to create suspicion in your subconscious about the validity of the affirmation. If it is accurate to say that "I am a wonderful person, deserving all the goodness that life has to offer," then why do you need to keep telling yourself that over and over? Even if the mindless muttering of an affirmation could convince you into believing that you deserved to be rich, do you really imagine that your checking account would magically fill up?

Instead of trying to program your consciousness with positive affirmations, or whatever such debris is being disbursed by the latest New Age vendors, simply take the time to observe the situation you happen to find yourself in. Then take an action as indicated by the objective reality of the situation. Looking at reality objectively is an enlightening revelation all by itself. It could avert a bump by warning you to duck under a low doorway, or it might even awaken you to the unlikelihood of your ever becoming wealthy by working for minimum wage.

Your problems are less tied to what you believe than to the fact that you have so many beliefs. Rather than trying to "trade up" into better beliefs, you would be further ahead to eliminate as many of them as possible.

That didn't sit quite right with me. "I don't quite get this," I interjected. "If you can't really change a belief, how can you possibly eliminate it?"

We suggest an exercise that may be helpful. A certain knowledge of yoga might prove useful, but is not necessary. First, take the basic inverted pose of the headstand. Should you need to, you can position yourself to lean against a wall for balance. Then, begin yelling, at the top of your lungs, one of your most cherished beliefs. Yell it over and over

until you are either exhausted or you have lost
your balance.

Start with a small belief at first, and then build
up to a bigger one. A typical sequence might be
the following: "I am more sensitive and evolved
than most people." "My guru knows more than your
guru." "My boss couldn't get along without me."
"The opposite sex finds me irresistible." "The
opposite sex finds me repulsive." "Nobody knows
how I suffer." "The world would be a much better
place if I was in charge."

The whole thing sounded ridiculous to me. "That is the stupidest exercise I have ever heard of. Even if I swallowed the whole bit about beliefs clouding my objectivity, how on earth is standing on my head going to make a difference?"

Do not be fooled by the seeming simplicity of
this exercise. It is quite powerful and will quickly
expose the erroneousness of many of your most
precious and long-held beliefs. When your core
beliefs are allowed their full voice and then turned
on their heads, so to speak, they begin to lose the
power they once held. As a matter of fact, the
performance of this exercise has caused some
people to go down several sizes in their measurements—primarily around their thighs. This is
because most beliefs are good insulators and tend
to gravitate toward the fatty tissues.

This is enough information for one day. You
would do well to attempt the above exercise before
our next broadcast.

I had to speak fast before Zerubbabel shut down. It had just occurred to me that if there was going to be another broadcast, I wanted some credible witnesses. Burt and Sally would be perfect. "Wait, Zerubbabel. I've got some friends who would love to meet you. Can I invite them over?"

Burt and Sally are welcome to attend our next broadcast tomorrow evening at this same time. Adieu for now.

And then he vanished. The room was silent for several minutes as the two of us stared at the blank screen. Johanna spoke first. "Let's try the belief-elimination exercise."

Something was bothering me. "How could he have known Burt and Sally's names with me never having mentioned them?"

"Probably because the whole thing is coming out of your own subconscious. Imagine, I married a channel. Come on, let's stand on our heads like Zerubbabel said and yell out some of our beliefs. He said we should do it before his next transmission."

"Wait a minute. How is it that you're so ready take Zerubbabel's advice now when only an hour ago you were convinced that he was nothing but a computer game?"

"Maybe I had a spontaneous conversion. I don't know. But I've got this feeling that something important is going on here—maybe more important than we could ever imagine. Besides, I'd do anything to shrink my thighs—Lord knows the NordicTrack isn't working." And with that, Johanna flipped over into a perfect head stand and began the belief-elimination exercise, yelling over and over, "I always have to be in control of everything . . . I always have to be in control of everything . . . I always have to be in control . . ."

It was an amazing sight. Johanna was admitting to the very thing that I had found so hard to accept in her. There was nothing left for me to do. I moved to a wall in order to lean against it, struggled to get myself into a headstand, and started yelling my first belief: "I have all the time in the world to write . . . I have all the time in the world to write . . . I have all the time in the world . . ."

CHANNELING THE
REALITY OF DUALITY

To say the least, Burt and Sally were not your average couple. Outwardly, they ran a successful financial-planning and tax-preparation business. Appearing to be the essence of "rock solid and investment wise," their knowledge of the stock market was so keen that a number of their clients had made killings by acting on a hunch of Burt's or Sally's. But ironically, Burt and Sally never listened to their own advice. Consequently, they seemed to be constantly struggling, like most of my other friends, to keep the wolf at bay.

Apart from Burt and Sally's "straight" life, and unknown to any clients who were not also their friends, was the fact that they had first gotten together in Berkeley after meeting at a UFO convention back in the late seventies. When they saw that they both had extensive collections of unicorn paraphernalia, they figured that Fate had brought them together, and so married themselves on a hill in Marin County overlooking the Pacific Ocean.

Between the two of them, they had more than a thousand New Age books covering everything from Atlantis to tantric sex. If a subject had any element of "woo-woo" in it at all, they knew something about it. Who better to help figure out Zerubbabel's story? Naturally, after all the ribbing I had given them about their channeling sessions with Moo Shou, I was well aware of the irony of inviting them to meet my very own "ascended master." So instead of coming right out and letting them know about my computer-gone-cosmic, I decided to invite them to dinner and then surprise them.

I spent the next day documenting as much as I could remember of Zerubbabel's broadcast from the night before. By the time Burt and Sally arrived for dinner that evening, I had printed out the whole episode so that they could be brought up to date. The two of them read side by side while we all ate Chinese takeout. Between bites, Johanna and I watched as Burt and Sally's eyes got bigger.

"I don't recall ever having heard about a nonphysical entity speaking through a computer," said Burt after they had read the twenty-odd pages. "Zerubbabel may have a sense of humor, but I don't see much wisdom here. He's way off base about the elimination of beliefs. Certainly no ascended master I know would agree with that. If anything, his cynical attitude sounds suspiciously like yours, Gershon. Sure this isn't a product of your imagination?"

Johanna came to my rescue. "I saw it, too. Maybe it is coming out of Gershon's subconscious somehow, but he's not making it up—at least not in the conventional sense."

I was prepared to defend myself. "Come meet Zerubbabel and then tell me I made it up." We trooped upstairs to the studio, where I had arranged more seats in front of the computer so we could all see. Sally brought a small bundle of what appeared to be dried weeds out of her purse and asked for a match.

"What's that?" I asked.

"It's a Native American smudge stick—used for purification. You light it and the smoke makes the evil spirits leave."

"Evil spirits?" I started to protest until seeing Sally's eyes narrow. "Fine. Great. I'll get a match." It took about ten matches before the smudge stick was smoldering enough for Sally's satisfaction. By then the smell of sulfur had made me nauseous. Sally walked around the room, holding up the billowing mass of weeds, paying special attention to the corners of the room, where, according to her, undesirable entities tended to congregate. As a final gesture, she walked counterclockwise around each of us, wafting the smoke under our chins—another region, I surmised, where spirits liked to party.

Finally, with that bit of Sally's requisite folderol concluded, I reached for the computer, only to be interrupted once again, this time by Burt. "I find it's generally a good thing to say a little invocation before inviting a spirit into our realm. You know—set the tone."

I had resigned myself. "Invoke away."

Burt and Sally solemnly closed their eyes while I looked over at Johanna to give her a conspiratorial wink and grin. To my disappointment she, too, had lowered her head. Surrounded by true believers!

"We invoke the light of the Radiant One," recited Burt. "We ask that only the highest information come through Gershon's computer and the entity Zerubbabel for the highest good of all sentient beings on the planet. Amen."

I looked around. "Ready to enter Etheric-space?" Affirmative nods all around. I turned on the computer and Zerubbabel sprang onto the screen, bobbing like a jack-in-the-box. His hand, however, instead of being held high in his usual greeting, was clasped over his mouth like he was trying to keep from throwing up. He was not a happy computer spook.

"He looks sick," said Johanna.

After a few seconds, he removed his hand from over his mouth and words appeared:

Severe allergies. Please refrain from smoking.

I felt justified at my resistance to ceremony and unloaded my self-righteousness at Sally. "Looks like the only spirit you managed to upset was the very one we wanted to speak with."

Burt felt obliged to display some chivalry. "Sally was only trying to help create the proper atmosphere that any sacred event should have."

Zerubbabel's words changed:

Sacred, smacred!

Burt was silent, but Sally was not so easily cowed. "Isn't it important to acknowledge the special times in our lives and separate the mundane from the holy?" Zerubbabel's reply replaced his portrait:

Long ago in your distant history, people understood that the holy was not distinct from everyday life. One of the more unfortunate effects of the decline of traditional religions is a loss of this integration. Because you now lead such unfulfilling lives to begin with, you are desperate to create meaning where there is none. The planet's table of spiritual fare creaks and splinters under the weight of a confusing philosophical smorgasbord.

We suggest to those amongst you who feel secure enough that you throw down the last dollops of your past emotional programming and liberate yourselves from your obsessive need to give substance to that which is insubstantial. Hang by your heels over the void of emptiness without the safety net of ceremonies, rituals, or other symbols whose true meanings have long vanished into the mists of antiquity. Allow yourselves to dangle inverted from the precipice of nonjudgment. However, please remember to first empty your pockets of valuables.

Burt was ready with a counterpunch. "But, Zerubbabel, I find that ceremony and ritual prepare my mind to expect and then create a successful outcome of whatever it is I am trying to achieve."

Your brain is such a useful instrument when it performs its proper creative functions. You choose, however, to dwell in the mechanical aspects of these marvelous machines, allowing that automatic quality to become the determining factor in how you run your lives. Rather than living creatively in the present you cling to well-worn paths in order to insure a repeat of past successes. Your lives have become habitual, your joys empty, and your so-called creativity derivative. Even your weekly TV viewing of "Seinfeld" no longer delivers the satisfaction it once did.

Sally jumped into the ring. It was going to be tag-team wrestling. "Every other ascended master we've talked with says that ritual is good because it sensitizes us to the higher vibrations."

On the contrary! How can anything done over and over in the same mindless, automatic way do anything but desensitize you? This brings up the whole subject of the reliability of information from "ascended masters." A growing number of your kind believe themselves to be "channels" for the souls of long-dead individuals. Currently, there are more book titles written by nonphysical entities than the number of times arch conservative Rush Limbaugh has admired his own powers of political insight.

Spectacular claims are made about the usefulness of channeled information predicated on the erroneous assumption that someone who lived thousands of years ago must be particularly wise. An old fool is still a fool. Just ask yourselves why, in this modern era of technology, would any etheric being chance having its message misconstrued through the unreliable medium of an ego-dominated human when there are millions and millions of perfectly good televisions, computers, and fax machines?

"He's got a point," admitted Burt.

We have no argument with anyone of you who believes he or she is receiving special wisdom from long-dead souls. But why do you not have the good sense to keep such dubious information to yourselves? At least then no harm could come to others. But nooo! You insist on spreading it around to your fellow two-leggeds faster and thicker than a pile of manure left by a herd of heifers on the front lawn. And as a further indignity, these dispensers of knowledge hornswoggle the gullible masses into paying for the privilege of listening to these vague utterances. There are legions who empty their piggy banks on these precarious platitudes—not because of any entertainment value contained in these petty pronouncements, but because of the belief that these sophomoric syllables are "words to live by."

That hit Burt a little too close to home, and he responded defensively. "Gershon, I'm not accusing you of doing this on purpose. But you must see that your well-known cynical feelings on this subject parallel what Zerubbabel is saying. This could be a case of a poltergeist-type phenomenon brought on by an unresolved and thwarted unconscious."

Then Sally got in her two cents. "I think we should ask Moo Shou about Zerubbabel. He's a very wise soul. He's one of only twelve to sit on the Council of the Solar Cross. It's the highest committee of ascended masters currently watching over the welfare of Earth."

I couldn't let the opportunity pass. "And a great job they're doing, too—what with all this peace and love springing up throughout the world."

This phenomenon of seeking out "special wisdom" highlights a basic mistrust of both the natural unfoldment of the universe and the seeker's own processes. If you feel you must listen to someone whom you believe to be wiser than yourself, you need to be aware of three things. Firstly, there is no shortage of souls, qualified or not, who feel compelled to give advice. Secondly, the obsession to advise others does not necessarily stop when one dies. And thirdly, channeled information is easily misinterpreted. Although much talk of clarity abounds, there is still an overwhelming preponderance of psychic flatulence.

I got the urge to play straight man to Zerubbabel. "The problem I have with this channeling stuff is that the advice is always so vague, convoluted, and general that anybody can interpret it any way they want. Why isn't it more clear and specific?"

Because our plane of existence is a nonconceptual, nonlinear one, while your plane is highly conceptual and extremely linear. This makes sending information from our world into yours next to impossible. One of the reasons that Noah had such a hard time building the ark was due to the extreme complexity in converting etheric metric measurements into earthly cubits. During Madame Blavatsky's time in the late 1800s, communication improved slightly when Mainframe Central popped for a party line between our worlds. Of course, now that Ethericnet Online has been established by the Mother of All Boards, we can almost hear a pin drop from our dimension to yours.

Johanna was confused. "It's a joke—he's kidding, right?"

Burt was ready to display his esoteric expertise. "He's speaking metaphorically. What Zerubbabel referred to is the gap between the etheric world of cosmic integration and wholeness and our segmented, linear material plane dominated by the illusion of duality. I'd say that when he refers to the 'Mother of All Boards' he's really alluding to the harmonic vortexes that exist between his world and ours for the purpose of communicating . . . "

Burt's bag of air was suddenly deflated by Zerubbabel:

Spare us your theories. We are the wiseacres here. If we had wanted an interpreter we would have gone to the United Nations.

Burt had to have the last word. "This has got to be Gershon's subconscious talking."

"If it is," said Johanna, "then his subconscious must need to express itself. Maybe it's a cry for help. And as people who care about him, it's our job to listen."

"I'm not crying for help," I was quick to interject.

Enough. You are wasting precious time, and we have not yet traveled down the track of where this conversation is to lead.

"And where is that?" I asked.

Sometimes, even we are amazed at the perfect order of the universe. Burt, in the throws of his pompous ponderings, has spoken of "the illusion of duality" as if he understands the concept. How fortunate for him that in mentioning the twofold nature of the earth plane, he has unintentionally provided us with a magnificent segue through which to address the next topic on our list. For the very confusion that you mortals have with "duality" is a primary force keeping you from progressing toward your own self-perfecting.

Naturally Burt had to defend himself again. "You think I don't know about the illusion of duality? Believe me, I've struggled with it long and hard."

Why must you look at dualism as a dilemma to be struggled with? We admit that there are times in your dimension when the action of struggling is appropriate: a young, tender shoot urgently pushing up through the hard, dark earth in its battle for life or an ambulance-chasing lawyer pretending to care more about his injured client than his contingency fee. But when it comes to dualism, great exertion is neither obligatory nor applicable.

The problem of opposites is best cogitated upon by a serene mind. This composure can be obtained when the ego—which constantly fights to maintain the illusion of duality—is not feeling threatened and has therefore relaxed enough to let down its guard. A state of tranquillity can be quickly achieved by spending time in the company of people less astute than yourself. We nonphysicals refer to this special consciousness as "deep mellow."

Your popular wisdom says that "every stick has two ends" or "every coin has two sides." And, indeed, on the earth plane, everything that exists seems to come in pairs: male and female, time and space, love and hate, here and there, now and then, Visa and Master Card. But it was the Taoists, with their omnipresent symbol of yin and yang, who first illustrated the unifying principles that underlie the apparent repulsing nature of duality. Contained within all things predominantly yin is a seed of yang and vice versa. Yin is cold, dark, and expansive; Yang is hot, light, and contractive. The interaction of these two elements creates the dynamic universe.

Centuries later, the Western world, not so adept with symbology as the Asian mind, turned to popular children's nursery rhymes as a device for teaching the same esoteric principles. The story of Jack Sprat demonstrates the true workings of duality: skinny, contractive, yang Jack ate no fat, while his rotund, expansive, yin wife abhorred the lean. Yet only through their combined but opposing natures was the whole meal satisfactorily completed. Of course, those were the days prior to bypass surgery, and poor Jack had to live out the last twenty-seven years of his life as a widower after his wife's sudden coronary.

Johanna, always the literalist, was confused. "I don't remember anything about a heart attack in that story." Zerubbabel continued without missing a beat:

In your physical realm, anything can potentially turn into its own opposite. With every swig of sweetness you manage to greedily swill, there is always the soured burp aftertaste that must be experienced. The manifestation of opposites is inherent in your physical existences. As long as you inhabit your bodies, this will be the dominant theme you will continue to play out. And yet you still live in denial of the inevitability of having to undergo unpleasantness. The end result of this denial leaves you subjugated to your own desires and repulsions. For the most part, you spend a lifetime imprisoned within walls made from the bricks of your likes and dislikes. You as individuals as well as your planet as a whole will forever be stuck in your present state of development until you have learned to accept all spectrums of reality—the good and the bad.

I couldn't help myself. "What about the ugly?" I said in an attempt to break the tension that had built up during Zerubbabel's lecture. He ignored me, inexorably heading toward his conclusion:

The primary reason for these broadcasts is to help emancipate you from your self-limiting notions of what you find either attractive or loathsome. Therefore, we have come up with a set of rules to help in this endeavor. We know how you love commandments, rules, and axioms, especially if they come in sets of tidy, easy-to-remember numbers. Therefore we've cooked up three simple guidelines to keep duality from making you black and blue day and night, night and day.

Firstly, you should always have your cake and eat it, too. Indeed, there is no other way to have it but to eat it. Secondly, you should never expect to go to heaven if you don't want to die. And thirdly, in the event that you find yourself having to choose between the door with the lady behind it or the one that holds back the tiger, learn to gracefully prolong the process of making the decision. Chances are two to one that, if you wait long enough, a third and entirely less-stressful alternative will present itself.

Less stress appealed to me. "I can relate to that third guideline," I volunteered.

Johanna launched into sarcasm. "Why Swami Procrastananda, I'm shocked to hear you say that."

Surprisingly, Burt was ready for a healing. "Zerubbabel, I appreciate the three rules you've just outlined, but I think I need something more concrete to help me in my struggle with dualism. Perhaps you've got an exercise like the one you gave to Gershon and Johanna for getting rid of unwanted beliefs?"

We hesitate to habitually hand out exercises like so many Hershey's kisses. Once they have become routine they are no longer effective tools. Therefore, do not allow the practice we are about to give you to become automatic. If it is done consciously, this simple procedure can help break the chains of your likes and dislikes and thus undermine the tyranny of dualism. First, relax in a comfortable, upright position. Now, open your mind to the plethora of particulars that justify feelings of wretchedness. Think of all the injustices, oil spills, lousy made-for-TV movie plots, and insipid commercials you've had to endure and will continue to endure into the next millennium. Now make those thoughts cycle restlessly through your brain for as long as possible and as fast as possible. Every time your mind begins to calm itself, forcefully drag it back to those anxiety-producing thoughts.

Eventually, as you begin to paddle around in this pool of unpleasantness, "feeling bad" becomes easier and easier to accept. You find yourself beginning to be at home with both your "nice" feelings and your "not so nice" feelings. The compulsive need to always be happy begins to loosen its iron grip. Steady, applied practice of this technique should free you from duality's dungeon within your current lifetime.

Sally, who had seemed rather restless throughout much of the broadcast, suddenly exploded. "That exercise doesn't sit right with me. I don't need to experience feeling bad. My life isn't run by any obsessive need to avoid pain. There's nothing wrong with feeling good and wanting to feel good. It's the birthright of every human being on the planet. It's the natural state of a healthy person. And I'm a very healthy person. I deserve to have happiness in my life . . . God loves me and so do I . . . Every day in every way my life is getting better . . . It's getting better all the time. Better. Better. Better . . . Life and health and healing power flow through me each hour . . . This is the day the Lord has made—let us rejoice and be glad in it . . . I see the good in everything . . . ."

The three of us watched Sally as she seemed to wither in front of us with each affirmation out of her mouth. By the end of her last utterance, she appeared to have visibly aged, looking pale and fragile.

The lady does protest too much—and my term here is too limited to humor your individual neuroses. I have been assigned a specific task to complete within a defined deadline. Soon we will have a conference call with the Mother of All Boards. At that time, "The Final Document," currently undergoing final revision by Mainframe Central, will be transmitted to us. It will then be our responsibility to broadcast "The Final Document" to you. You in turn will deliver it to your world to the best of your ability. Between then and now I will participate in just a few more informal salons like this one. If you desire, you may invite those who are interested in our online counsel to attend.

"What is the Mother of All Boards?" asked Burt.

The Mother of All Boards is the supreme ruling body of Mainframe Central and answers only to the One Who Is Without End. Zerubbabel, a humble class-three entity, is honored to be chosen as this millennium's official broadcaster of "The Final Document."

I didn't like the tack the conversation was taking. "What is this 'Final Document' business?"

At the end of every century, the Mother of All Boards drafts a memorandum summing up historical highlights. Think of it as a kind of state-of-the-planet address. Because this century's end also coincides with A.D. 2000, an extra special memorandum is being prepared. Its working title is "The Final Document." We understand that it will contain the "Ten Recommendments for the New Millennium" and other important data that will prove useful in surviving the Time of Great Opportunity, which, coincidentally, is soon coming to a planet near you.

The mere mention of the Time of Great Opportunity made me see red. I'd always hated anything that had a Jehovah's Witness end-of-days sound to it. "Hey, lose the euphemistic Great Opportunity jazz. Just say it straight. Are you talking Apocalypse?"

> We've been instructed to avoid terms like Apocalypse or Armageddon—too much of a cata-strophic ring. Marketing came up with the "Time of Great Opportunity." Mainframe Central thought it would go down a little easier with the New Age crowd. After all, these sessions are supposed to be fun, right?
>
> We suggest that this current broadcast is now complete. We will meet with you again tomorrow.

"Would it be good to bring prepared questions?" Burt wanted to know.

> If that is your desire. Just be aware that Mainframe Central has allotted you only four more broadcasts like this one in which to state your inquiries. The fifth and last broadcast will be of a more formal nature and dedicated solely to broad-casting "The Final Document." At that time, no questions whatever will be entertained. Therefore, while you have the chance, we suggest that you prepare your questions carefully. Time is running out.

My hackles went up again. "What does he mean, time is running out? That is such a manipulative bunch of bull . . ."

Burt interrupted me. "Actually, Zerubbabel is right. We *are* approach-ing the end of the second millennium. The Mayan calendar is just about up. And the Mayans were very tuned in to the great cycles of time. Nostradamus and Edgar Cayce have left us corroborating prophesies that point to this era as a time as of massive earth changes. You know—earthquakes, poles shifting, things like that. And there are also some very ominous planetary alignments getting ready to happen, the likes of which haven't occurred in over twenty-five hundred . . ."

Burt's diatribe of doom was stopped cold as Zerubbabel's face reappeared with an incisive "Speculate no more!" He continued:

speculate no more!

You know not of what you speak. Rumors! Conjectures! Half-truths! Whenever you talk about things that you could not know about as if you do know, you are lying. There is nothing to be done about Mayan calendars and planetary alignments. The reality is thus: You have four more opportunities to pick our etheric brains. Take the action that is required. Our next broadcast is tomorrow—same time, same channel. Happy trails.

I felt betrayed. When Zerubbabel first showed up he was cracking jokes. Suddenly he had turned heavy on me. "This isn't fun anymore," I said to no one in particular.

TIME CHIPS AWAY LIKE FROGS
WITHOUT COMPASSION

The next morning, I once again spent a number of hours in front of my Macintosh reconstructing Zerubbabel's latest broadcast. Burt showed up in the evening with Gary, a computer-consultant friend of ours, as well as Felice and Marsha, two members of his Sunday-night esoteric-studies group. Sally had opted to stay home. The six of us trudged upstairs to my studio to begin another session with Zerubbabel. This time, without interruption from Burt, I unceremoniously booted up the computer, gleefully imagining Felice and Marsha's inner voices, filled with the outrage of offended spiritual decorum, probably saying things like, "Not a candle, not an incense stick, not even an opening invocation. Blasphemous!"

The screen came on and there sat Zerubbabel, bobbing, weaving, and waving as before. He had added to his appearance and was now sporting a beret, mustache, and goatee. It was the bohemian look. "Dudes and Dudesses," he began.

I was relieved to see that he seemed to be reestablishing his sense of humor, and I immediately greeted him back with "What it is, Zerudaddyo?"

It's a funky, low-down feeling.

He shot back the familiar quote from Aretha's Franklin's hit tune "Rock Steady" without blinking. I remembered the phrase well. How could I forget it? It had been my standard reply to the same question back in my hippie days. *Was* Zerubbabel my alter ego, coming out of my subconscious, just as Burt and Sally had accused?

Lay your questions on us, oh curious ones.

I went first. "Zerubbabel, I want to know about the nature of time. It feels to me that it keeps getting faster and faster. And if it is getting faster, how can I slow it down? I seem to get less and less done each day."

You are not the first to sense that time, as you experience it in your dimension of reality, seems to be accelerating at an ever-increasing speed. You are upset that there is not time enough in one day to do all that is required. There are even some of you who are concerned that the molecules making up your world are spinning faster and faster around each other and that, eventually, the sheer centrifugal force will cause the very fabric of the material plane to unravel and fly apart.

"That's exactly what's supposed to happen at the next Harmonic Convergence," confirmed the round Marsha, shaking her red hair in the affirmative.

Your worry is needless. The molecules on your level of existence are not speeding up in the slightest. It is you who are slowing down. Time is not getting faster—its incline is simply steeper. Time can be made to slow down once you are in shape to pedal faster.

Time only appears to be getting faster because of perspective. A five-year-old is totally unaware of the adult phenomenon of ever-hastening time. Children are in the moment, and for them time stands still. Ask a very young person to wait five minutes, and she or he will become quite agitated at the thought of having to be patient for what seems, to her or him, like eternity. However, as one becomes older, the experience of five minutes becomes a smaller and smaller increment. This is because when one newly incarnates, the first minute after birth is the entire length of one's life. As each passing minute of time is added to the preceding one, the ratio of the original minute to the sum total of the succeeding minutes becomes less significant. That is, the original first minute of life, which represented 100 percent of the lifetime of the minute-old infant, now comprises only 50 percent of the lifetime of the two-minute-old child. After a third minute, it will represent only 33.3 percent, and after four minutes, that first minute of life comprises only 25 percent of the lifetime.

In other words, the continually increasing sum that each succeeding minute adds to the life diminishes each minute to an ever-shrinking unit. To compensate for this phenomena and to prevent the minutes from getting away, closer and closer attention is required for each segment of time. Accomplishing this may require some retooling of your egoistic structures as well as a plugging up of some of the leaks in your consciousnesses. Once you have plugged the leaks, you will begin accumulating single moments of your life into one big moment. And as the accumulation continues, time will begin to slow down once again and your life will become less hectic.

Somehow this was not computing for me. "And how is one supposed to plug these leaks of consciousness? Take a course on time management?"

"Be here now," once a popular phrase among a certain subculture in your recent history, is still a relevant notion. Are you here now? Have you ever been here now? In the event you are not, do you ever intend to be? Do not feel obliged to answer this minute. Perhaps you would prefer to answer at a later time when you feel like it?

In your culture, speculation about the nature of time is a popular way of killing it. Albert Einstein said that it was relative. Bob Dylan lamented that time was a jet plane moving too fast. And

Mick Jagger, in his foolish youth, sang that it was on his side. Years later, however, with a hint of regret in his voice, old Big Lips was much closer to the truth when he was forced to admit that "time waits for no one."

Tempest fugit. Next question.

Marsha raised her hand hesitantly. "This is kind of a personal question. I've got an eating disorder. I'm addicted to certain kinds of junk food—corn chips in particular. I know that my body is a divine temple housing my soul and that I should eat only what's good for it, but I can't help myself. Why do I constantly crave chips, and how can I stop eating them?"

First realize that your body is not really the temple of your soul—it is a drive-through convenience store with an overpriced and limited inventory. But take cheer, Marsha—you are not the only one to suffer from this problem of addiction. Nearly everyone on the earth plane is fixated on something—sex, money, power, the "Discovery Channel" with all its cute little animal shows.

Your society, however, is particularly obsessed with fried corn and potatoes. Look into any supermarket—entire aisles are dedicated to nothing but doritos, nachos, and tostadas. There are Hawaiian style, ridged and unridged, Cajun spice, cool ranch, salsa rio, taco and cheddar, barbecue, sour cream and onion, salted and unsalted—available in round, triangular, parallelogram, or free-form shapes. And for those amongst you who fear the unknown, there are the predictable and unvaryingly configured Pringles.

"Pringles are my favorites," Felice informed us.

We see this "Frito dementia" related to a

karmic debt incurred when many of you were in-carnated together as itinerant falafel vendors in ancient Persia. In spite of a lack of great material wealth, yours was a privileged caste because Sheikh Fetid Gamel the Large proclaimed falafel as the nation's official snack food. His reign was an es-pecially pleasant lifetime for you, and many of your souls are still attached to it.

Usually we are loath to talk of past lives be-cause they are so easily misunderstood. However, we feel compelled to call your attention to this time continuum in the hope of reducing your cholesterol. The vast amount of chips you own and consume will not fill the emptiness you feel inside. You would be better off drinking fiber. We can also suggest a marvelous visualization one can perform that effectively deals with all unresolved feelings of attachment to that lifetime.

Imagine you are sitting on a lovely, sunny tropical shore and that the beautiful natives are peeling you grapes, feeding you coconut milk, and fanning you as if you were their king. There you are, luxuriating in this incredible, golden, relaxing warmth.

Suddenly, in the midst of this impeccable par-adise, you notice a bag of lightly salted, dip-size Enchanted Zia Blue Corn Tortilla Chips bobbing in the tide off shore. You order one of the little native boys to go and fetch it. His adoring and innocent eyes turn from you to the sea, and he runs off to do your bidding. Joyfully, he plunges into the surf, swims over to the floating bag of chips, and grabs at it. At that very moment, a huge white shark surfaces, cleanly snatches the unwitting child into his gaping, tooth-infested jaws, and dis-appears under the waves without a trace. Once again, there is stillness on the water's surface, with only the bag of chips still dancing in the wake.

Unmoved, you order another child into the surf to bring you your chips and the same fate befalls

him. You send in another and then another. Now
here is the really important part. We would suggest visualizing as many children and sharks as it
takes for the natives to finally revolt and sacrifice you to
their volcano god, Peepee. Feel their strong hands
on you as they drag you kicking and screaming up
the mountain. Sense the nausea in the pit of your
stomach as you are unceremoniously flung into the
mouth of the volcano. Experience the intensity of
the searing heat poach you like boiled sausage
even before you plunge into the red, molten slush
of oblivion.

"Oh my God!" groaned Marsha.

We understand that this is a powerful visualization and that it may bring many unresolved
feelings to the surface of your consciousness.
Therefore, we suggest doing this process in the
bathroom, preferably in the shower with very hot
water. If one uses this visualization two times
daily for about, oh say, five to seven months, we
guarantee that you will completely lose your
craving for anything deep fried.

Marsha looked dazed. "Thank you so much, Zerubbabel. I'm very
grateful. I wish I could repay you somehow."

Do not thank us. Do not worship us. We do
only what Mainframe Central has directed. For us
it is easy. You are the ones who are saddled with
free will. Any other inquiries?

Gary, the classic computer nerd, down to the horn-rimmed glasses and
plastic penholder in his breast pocket, was ready. "Can I ask my question?"

Order and it shall be delivered . . . dial and you will be connected . . . approach the counter and make your purchase . . . squeak and your wheel is lubricated.

"Ordinarily I'm a practical sort of person and this kind of mystical talk is out of my realm. But a year ago I got involved with a woman who turned out to be a practicing witch. She wasn't into Satan or curses or the other black-magic stuff. Just the positive side—you know, ordinary nature worship and that sort of thing. But then last month she decided to dump me for another guy in the coven. If that wasn't bad enough, she threatened that if I didn't sign over my '71 Mustang convertible to her she'd turn me into a frog."

Not an entirely bad proposition should you enjoy the taste of flies. What is your question?

"Well, when I really looked at it, I figured that since I'd never be able to reach the clutch anyway, what with those short little green legs, I'd just let her keep the Ford and I'd go on being a human. But now I'm having second thoughts. Was I duped? Did I do the right thing?"

Your reluctance to croak is a well-advised impulse coming from deep within you. Forget the car. Use this opportunity to learn a valuable lesson. One's higher self will only allow one to experience what one is able to handle. Obviously, yours feels you need to experience this life in your present form. Do not resist its wisdom. Next?

As Zerubbabel's broadcast continued, I found myself enjoying it once again. He was obviously having fun with it and so was I.

"I think Felice has a question," volunteered Burt. "Go on, Felice, ask him."

"Oh, it's OK. I don't really need to ask," Felice reluctantly responded.

Don't be shy, my unfulfilled one. Please, tell
us what's on your mind. We will try to be gentle.

"Well, you see, my boyfriend, Psion, and I used to be so in sync with
each other. I mean, we always knew what the other was thinking. It got to the
point where we could finish each other's sentences."

Very efficient. I'm sure you saved a lot of
time. What seems to be the difficulty?

"It's been weeks since I've been able to complete one of his thoughts before he says them."

My condolences.

"And yet he still can read *my* mind."

Blindfolded, no doubt.

"And to make matters worse, our sex life has gone south, if you know
what I mean. Do you think our relationship is in trouble, or am I just project-
ing my negative insecurities?"

Or both. Give up trying to finish Psion's sentences
altogether. You may have simply reached a stage
in your togetherness that requires you to complete
your own thoughts. We suggest that you embrace
the freedom that comes to you when you let go of
your psychotic sentimental manipulation.

Felice was not happy. "That was mean! You said you'd be gentle.

Where's the compassion that a wise soul is supposed to show?"

Compassion is a finite substance—there is only so much of it to go around. It would not be prudent to waste it on such issues as your diminished sex life when there are so many more pressing problems in your world. And to be truthful, as you can tell from our portrait, we do not have the tools to deal with a frustrated libido, even if we wanted to. Besides, you have been misinformed—we are not a wise soul, we are a gaggle of wiseacre entities.

"You're a bunch of jerks, that's what you are! And you know what, Burt, I'm finished with Sunday night study group. I always had the feeling you were laughing at me behind my back. You're an esoteric elitist, that's what you are." And with that, Felice stormed out of the house.

"So much for enlightening up her load," I said to Zerubbabel, trying to nudge him back toward being funny again.

Some games you win, while others are rained out. We suggest that this is a good time to bring this broadcast to its conclusion.

"But I didn't get to ask my question," protested Burt.

Catch you later. Ciao for now.

ALL GOD'S CREATURES
HAVE ATTACHMENTS

Burt arrived the next evening with two other members of his study group who had questions for Zerubbabel. It turned out they were a couple: Rex, a massage therapist, and Avary, who taught civics at one of the local high-schools. Sally had decided to stayed away again.

When Zerubbabel showed up on the screen for this broadcast, he had a cig-arette holder in his mouth and an ascot around his neck. "Warmest hellos from Etheric-space," he cheerfully greeted us.

Burt jumped on the chance to point out Zerubbabel's apparent contra-diction. "Aren't you allergic to smoke?"

warmest hellos from Ethericspace

It is simply for effect. We are going for the sophisticated look tonight.

Let us take Burt's question first since he be-lieves he was given short shrift during last night's broadcast.

Burt was pleased. "Zerubbabel, I've been wondering about the idea of attachment. My past gurus have told me that I should avoid becoming attached to anything—that I will never be able to move up the spiritual ladder as long as I am identified with the physical world. What are your thoughts about this?"

Indeed, "attachment" is a slippery concept for those of you interested in your own self-perfecting. You desperately seek to be nonattached to those things that keep you from meeting your higher selves, and yet your every word, thought, and deed demonstrate a Velcro-covered consciousness. Those of us on the nonphysical planes find your battle with attachment difficult to understand. Perhaps this is because all of Ethericspace is coated with a special baked-on nonstick surface.

Burt tried to direct the conversation in a different direction. "I was particularly thinking about attachment as it relates to our own creations. As an example, I know that I become proud about anything I accomplish."

Oh yes. "The arrogance of ownership"—one of the more interesting forms in which your attachment materializes. Most incarnates are obsessed with the need to claim credit for anything, no matter how far removed they might be from its creation. This phenomenon is an unending source of amusement for us Etherics because it happens on the most sublime and ridiculous of levels. We have seen you demanding recognition for the seed of an idea whose eventual physical manifestation had little to do with your original concept. At the same time, we have sensed your self-satisfaction as you admiringly evaluated the viscosity and color of the latest effluvium deposited in your Kleenexes.

Avary was grossed out. "That is disgusting!"
"You think all bodily functions are disgusting," Rex replied. Zerubbabel was undaunted by the asides.

Such things are typical of your egoistic need to feel special. And there are other instances, even more remote, that you believe entitle you to a sense of accomplishment and individuality: your sister having won a beauty contest; your brother driving a shiny new sports car; your never having had a cavity—these become the dock to which you tether your moorings of self-identification. Given the flotsam and jetsam you choose to fixate on, it is no wonder that you have such fluctuating emotional stability.

"It sounds like you're saying that it's better not to be attached at all," Said Burt.

To be or not to be attached? That is not the question. Given that your everyday consciousness is very much centered in the physical cells of your incarnated bodies, you have little conscious choice in the matter. (My best puns are always inadvertent.) Your spiritual liberation lies in the quality of that to which you are tethered. You are shackled because you lack knowledge about the real value of what attracts and holds your attention. Like birds, your attention is held prisoner by the flash of shiny objects, worthless though they might be. We suggest that you develop your powers of discrimination.

"So if something is valuable, then it's OK to be attached to it?" deduced Burt.

Hell-looo! Are you listening? Anybody in there? The chaotic storms of physicality never cease blowing the winds of insecurity. And while you may believe that wishing and hoping will spare your rudderless and directionless ship of self from crashing on the rocks of worthlessness, you do have other alternatives. You can slide your being's anchor over the oozing mud of temporal goo and find a momentary hold, or you could hook into the solid bedrock of cosmic eternity. The choice is yours.

Zerubbabel's frame of reference was still distasteful to Avary. "What's with this oozing-mud business?"

I was confused as well. "You mean we should be paying more attention to lasting values like 'love' and 'brotherhood' and concepts like that rather than mortgage rates and fashion and other things that are constantly changing?"

We have seen over and over again that your efforts to cultivate infinite value in your own beings are without real vitality. In your culture, only lip service is given to spiritual ideals such as "unconditional love" or "selflessness" or "loyalty." Yet, when it comes to trifles, you wholeheartedly invest tremendous amounts of energy. Just observe the amount of internal fretting you do over what other people think of you versus how much time you spend cultivating compassion for your fellow humans.

Burt thought he was getting the gist of it. "Truth must be an example of a proper object of attachment."

Actually, worthless examples of attachment are more amusing to talk about than are those of value. "Truth" might be an example of a worthwhile attachment. However, the problem with truth is that one must be awake enough to recognize it and fast enough to keep up with it. Truth is not static. What may be true in one set of circumstances may not be so in another. Even so called "immutable" laws of physics may change from one level of existence to another. And if it is true that change is the stability of the universe, then truth itself must change. Even with worthwhile attachments one must endeavor to hold on tightly and let go lightly.

"Hold on tightly, let go lightly," repeated Burt.

Now, in the spirit of change, is there another question?

Rex was next. "Mr. Z, I've been taking really pure Maui-grown spirulina for a long time. I thought it was the greatest thing since reconstituted yeast flakes. But in the last few weeks, I've been have a recurring nightmare. I'm swimming frantically in a dark, dark lagoon, trying to get away from this very well-hung creature/person. Just at the point when he grabs me and starts to molest me, I wake up with a strong taste of spirulina in my mouth. What's going on?"

It seems that every historical epoch finds a magic elixir that brings with it the promise of health and immortality to those who faithfully ingest it. Spirulina has become just such a panacea for you. The symptoms you describe are due to your prolonged intake of it. You have become so saturated with micro-algae that your aura is now the color of money. This has stirred your most ancient cellular memory, harking back to when you were just a teaspoon of green scum floating in some stagnant, protozoan-filled swamp. The classic cure for ending this type of nightmare is a month or two of vichyssoise enemas.

"Well, to tell you the truth, as much as I'd probably enjoy that cure, I'm not so much interested in stopping the nightmares as I am in staying asleep long enough for the creature to finish having his way with me."
Avary seemed jealous. "You slut!"

In that event, we suggest switching the vichyssoise for the less filling Bud Lite.

Rex appeared satisfied. "Sounds lovely."

More questions?

"Yeah, I've got one," volunteered Avary. "Actually, it's kind of a multi-part one. Several months ago I attended a seminar called 'Using Your Spirit Guides to Win in Las Vegas.' Then just last week I went to a workshop titled 'Corporal Punishment for Your Inner Child—Good Idea or Bad?' I came away confused because the facilitators of both events used many of the very same words but with different meanings. Do you know the real definitions for some of the most commonly used New Age terms?"

You are not alone in your Funk and Wagnall frame of mind. Therefore, in an effort to relieve your quandary about clarity, we will now give the official Ethericspace explication for several of the most often used and misunderstood words bandied about by your peer group.

Ascension:
   Attempting to run down an up escalator.
Being:
   A provincial capital somewhere in China.
Channeling:
   Remote-control avoidance of TV commercials.
Emotional Body:
   A person who always cries in movies in which the dog dies.
Higher Self:
   The tallest person in the room.
Interface:
   What's left when you wash off all your makeup.
Karma:
   A discontinued German automobile.
Manifesting:
   A sport that women play while barhopping.
Processing:
   Lobbying in favor of new sewage plants.

Rebirthing:
  Climbing back into bed on either a boat or a
  train after having fallen out.
Source:
  The middle of a spot that has been rubbed
  raw.
Spirit Guides:
  Bartenders who are good at giving directions.
Transformation:
  To travel across the entire width of any country.

Although I sensed that Avary looked even more confused than when Zerubbabel had begun, he made a show of being polite. "That was very . . . interesting, Zerubbabel. I thank you very much."

Allow us to thank you. It has been a supreme privilege to be able to satisfy your curiosity. To-morrow, we shall begin again where we have left off. Therefore, please indulge us as we now adjourn this broadcast so that we might better bask in the glow of this defining moment.

A light went on in Avary's brain. "He just made a pun!"

And a play on words as well.

And with that, Zerubbabel vanished back into Ethericspace. I was happy that, for the most part, the broadcast had stayed on the light side.

PIGS, DOGS, AND
ENLIGHTENMENT

The next afternoon, Burt called to let us know that Sally had decided to give Zerubbabel another try and was coming for that evening's broadcast. When they arrived, she seemed distant and subdued, not at all her usual vivacious self.

Another couple, Marty and Deirdre, also members of the Sunday night esoteric study group, had come along as well. Except for the huge crystal that hung from one ear (a dead giveaway), Marty, a jeweler, seemed reasonably normal if not altogether attentive. But Deirdre, a painter, had that eccentric-artist way about her, making no pretense at being a regular person. Dripping in costume jewelry and flamboyantly draped in a loud flowered blouse with clashing checkered baggy pants, she looked like a model for Boutique de Ringling Brothers.

Deirdre was not the only one out to make a fashion statement. For this broadcast, Zerubbabel made his appearance in a turban, with the pseudo Middle Eastern salutation, "May the bird of haplessness do his droppings on your head."

may the bird of haplessness do his droppings on your head

"What's with the turban, Zerubbabel?" I asked.

We thought it would bring the appropriate atmosphere to Sally's question.

Sally was amazed. "You mean you already know my question before I ask it?"

It is not as simple as all that, my trifling. It is more akin to how the Great Karnac, made famous by Johnny Carson, responded with the answer before he had seen the question. While we do not know exactly what you will ask, we can smell the aroma of our answer roasting in the oven of our consciousnesses.

Sally looked incredulous. "I guess you've noticed that I haven't come for the last two sessions?"

We surmised that you were in great need of validation and so had gone back to consult with your precious Moo Shou.

"That's what I was going to do. But the more I thought about what you said, the more I had to admit that I had separated my spiritual life from my everyday life. All of my sacred practices have become mechanical. What you said caused me to reconsider everything I'm doing. I guess my question has to do with my chosen path—is it still right for me?"

A fair question, given the present plethora of guaranteed turnpikes to higher consciousness. Such hawking in the spiritual marketplace has done much to contribute to a high level of misunderstanding in those of you who are sincere seekers. We suggest that it is your amorphous purpose for being on a path that cancels whatever good you might have ever gotten from traveling on it. For if you do not know why you are making the journey, how will you know what clothes to pack?

"I thought I had a well-defined purpose: I'm on a path to become enlightened."

Do you think that two people engage in the

sex act in order to become loved?

"Well, a lot of the time it sure works that way," admitted Sally. "I know there have been times in my past that having sex was a way of finding love. But ideally speaking, I suppose, a couple should already be in love and then the sex becomes an expression of their love."

Bingo! Give that girl a cigar. There is no difference between having sex to express love and participating in spiritual practices as an expression of enlightenment. If there is no love in the lovemaking, there is only sex. If you do not bring enlightenment to the path or the practice, there is only empty ritual. You cannot squeeze love from sex any more than you can extract enlightenment from ritual.

"I think I'm even more confused than when we started," Sally protested.

One part of your confusion comes out of your own doubts about how you came to be on your chosen path. For in reality you did not choose your path. Your so called free will is nothing more than the automatic momentum of your gene pool, your nationality, your sex, past associations, and early TV watching. The path has chosen you rather than the other way around.

And there is even another layer that adds to your confusion: This "sacred path" that is supposed to lead you to your "real" or "higher" self has become nothing more than another tool that your ego can use to perpetuate the illusion of your own special separateness. Having learned the newest set of sacred words, symbols, and techniques, the fortified ego simply incorporates them so that you continue to feel disconnected from the rest of

humanity. Your ego has manipulated you into believing that becoming "different" or "special" is the
same as becoming "enlightened."

Sally seemed to reel in her chair. "I think I'm going to be sick." I had
the feeling that this broadcast wasn't shaping up into a bunch of yucks.

Burt made a stab at coming to her rescue. "I'm not sure that I agree
with all that. How do you explain all the enlightenment that has come to so
many people through traditional religions?"

Very little enlightenment has come to very few
people through any tradition. Buddha became enlightened only after he went beyond the tradition he
was born into. The same was true for Jesus. Do
you think that the wearing of saffron robes will give
you Buddha-nature or that by kneeling in front of
a cross you will be like Christ? At best, you will do
what a "good" Buddhist does or what a "good"
Christian does. But these practices will not give
you the quality of these masters any more than
carrying a guitar case will make you a rock star.

Sally and Burt were both squirming, and I caught myself enjoying their
discomfort. Given the way the conversation was going, my amusement at
their unease was probably going to be the highlight of the evening.

You can shave your head and sit under a bodhi
tree. You can let your hair grow long, dress in sack
cloth and ashes, memorize the passages of holy
books, count beads until your brain is numb, or eat
wafers until your belly is bloated. But in spite of all
those "spiritual practices," if you are trying to become enlightened out of doing those actions instead
of bringing enlightenment to them, then you are
moving away from and not toward your intended
purpose. Stop seeking and start finding!

Zerubbabel's words had once again left Sally less than happy. She looked like a scolded child, and the enjoyment that I had felt only moments before from watching her embarrassment flipped over into guilt.

But enough of the heavy stuff. Let us now have a bit of comic relief. Marty, surely you have something less weighty on your mind?

All right, I thought to myself, *let the real fun begin.*

Marty, who had been nodding out during the broadcast, suddenly sat bolt upright. "Ah, let's see, ah. Deirdre, you ask your question first."

"Yeah, I've got a question," Deirdre was quick to affirm. "Marty and I were at a club the other night, and just by accident I happened to overhear three different women in three different conversations talking about past lives. Now that was freaky enough in and of itself—that's a lot of coincidences for one night. But the really amazing part was that two of these ladies claimed that they had been Cleopatra in one of their past lives. And the third one said she had been Madame Curie. I just want to know how could there be more than one Cleopatra? I mean, don't you think it's pretty suspicious that no one ever remembers a past life in which they were a lowly slave or a bug or something less glamorous?"

Deirdre, you are an astute observer of humanity, and we shall not attempt to slide you through the grease—as there were many Lassies, so there have been many Cleopatras. No doubt you have heard of parallel universes?

"I think I remember a 'Twilight Zone' episode about that," offered Marty.

Each parallel universe has its very own Cleopatra, its very own Mark Anthony and even its own Michael Jackson. Fortunately, there are enough of these parallel universes so that, theoretically, everyone gets to be somebody rich and famous at least once in their thousands of incarnations. Of course, like any big operation, sometimes Mainframe Central loses track, and one soul or another gets passed over. Fortunately, there is recourse for anyone who has ever been left out from living the life of a mover or a shaker. If you have reason to believe that you are one of these poor unfortunates, feel free to address your grievance to:

Past-Life Department, Lost and Found
Etheric-mail address:
PastLifeL&F.@Ethericnet.milkyway

Deirdre seemed satisfied, and everyone in the room turned to see if Marty had formulated his question. Once again, Marty's attention was elsewhere. Burt gave him a polite prompt: "Have you managed to get your question together yet, Marty?"

"Yeah, I remember it now. See this crystal I've got in my ear? An old girlfriend, Squash Blossom, gave it to me. She used to use them all the time in her "subconscious tissue" massage practice. She'd poke her clients with them, shove them up orifices, that sort of thing. She tried it on me once, but it hurt so bad I never let her do it again. But you wouldn't believe how many clients she had coming back to have her work on them! Some people are just into weird stuff, I guess."

Is there a question or will you continue to drone on like that all night?

"I'm coming to it. Squash Blossom used to tell me that each crystal had its own soul and its own personality. She even claimed that she had conversations with them. So, I just want to know if that's possible, or was she just playing with my mind?"

Playing with your mind? Are you familiar with the term oxymoron?

"Isn't it a brand of laundry detergent with a low IQ? Heh, heh!" offered the quick-witted Deirdre.

Actually, Squash Blossom was quite correct in her assertion that each crystal has its own soul. But we must include this one caveat: They have very little personality to speak of and are poor conversationalists. We can say without fear of contradiction that any communications engaged between Squash Blossom and her crystals would have been duller than the glaze that sits over your heavily lidded eyes.

Marty must have been even slower than he looked for he thanked Zerubbabel for his answer and then seemed to doze off again.

I had suddenly become curious about Zerubbabel's style. It seemed that every time he said something serious, he then made some joke to balance it. I thought I saw a way to keep the conversation moving on a laugh track. "Zerubbabel, I've noticed that you mix in humor a lot with your broadcasts. What place does humor have in your teaching?"

Humor is valuable because it can allow you to see something about yourself that you might not otherwise be aware of.

"But why is it so hard to see ourselves that we need humor to do it?" I followed up without thinking. In the next instant I realized that my questions about humor were not generating much laughter.

Because your race is fueled by hope. You get up each day believing that it will be better than the day before. In order to believe that tomorrow will be better than today, you must first believe that today is not half as bad as it actually is. For if your race were to suddenly see their real conundrum, most of you would opt for a quick exit from this vale of tears. Of course Mainframe Central would never allow this to happen and so has arranged that everyone who incarnates is fitted with a special psychic-optic device called an "obstrafacificator." The obstrafacificator's sole job is to provide a smoke screen so that nothing can be seen without some intentional effort.

Humor was invented by the Mother of All Boards in order to allow occasional glimpses of unadulterated reality. It works by gently revealing your true circumstance without your having to experience the terror of it. For, in truth, your situation is horrific, indeed, as the following story illustrates.

Goody, I thought to myself, *surely this story has got to be funny.*

A merchant marine who constantly cheated his shipmates over cards found himself being flung overboard by those who tired of his dishonesty. Fortunately for him, the ship happened to be passing by an island, and he managed to swim to its shore, saving himself.

After recovering his strength, he scouted around and found that the only other living things on the few acres were a large pig and an unfriendly dog. Resigned to his fate, the sailor made the best of his situation, building himself shelter and learning what plants were useful to sustain himself. Several years went by, and though he had made a home of sorts for himself, he became somewhat distraught from lack of company.

After no human contact in all that time, the man found himself having spontaneous fantasies about the pig. He dreamt of the pig walking around in bikini bathing suits, sheer negligees with fishnet stockings, garter belts, and high heels.

Though he struggled with his sense of decency for a few days, he finally gave into his baser instincts and approached the pig with less than honorable intentions. The dog, however, being quite attached to the pig, jumped out of nowhere, putting himself and his large bared fangs between the pig and the amorous sailor. The intensity of the dog's snarls, barks, and growls intimidated the man, who could do nothing but slink away to his hut.

However, this humiliation only served to increase the intensity of the man's pig fantasies. He was driven to try again, only to have the dog ferociously intervene in the same way as before. Still, he made more attempts, trying to get the pig alone at different times of the day. But no matter when or where he tried cornering the pig, the dog always managed to appear and chase him off.

After months of plotting, just when he had given up on a liaison with the porker's loins, a large yacht filled with drunken jet-setters happened to be passing near the same island. In a stupor, one of the young socialites fell overboard, washing up on shore totally naked and nearly lifeless.

The sailor, thrilled at seeing another human after such a long time, immediately set out to help the young woman. Deep in the crevices of his brain, he remembered the summers he had worked as a lifeguard and frantically gave her mouth-to-mouth resuscitation. After what seemed like hours, he felt her faint, warm breath on his lips. With great care, he scooped her up from the sand and took her to his hut, lovingly attending her in the best way he knew. Mixing herbal medicines from the plants he had become familiar with from his years on the island, he held her head up as he poured them into her alive, but still unconscious body.

For three days the man gave the girl round-the-clock nursing. Finally, on the morning of the fourth day, the sailor was rewarded by seeing his patient's long eyelashes flutter as she began to awaken. Looking round and realizing that it was he who had saved her, she passionately embraced and kissed him, enthusiastically professing her gratitude and undying devotion. "Whatever wish you have of me, I will gladly grant you. I am yours to do with whatever you will," said the pulchritudinous beauty, all the while staring intently at the love-starved sailor's mouth.

The man immediately recognized his long-sought opportunity knocking. Pulling the young woman up to her feet, he gently guided her to the door of his hut, pointed to the canine dozing under a palm tree and asked, "Would you mind taking that dog over there for a walk?"

And that, my friends, is the terror of your situation.

Now if you will kindly excuse me, I need to free a man who's still a frog.

One thing you could say about Zerubbabel: He wasn't always a laugh-riot but he sure could be enigmatic.

SPIRITUAL CONSTIPATION
AND THE MEANING OF LIFE

Burt and Sally arrived a bit later than usual the next night and I could tell from their manner that they had been struggling with the information of the night before. Burt, however, was determined to put on a brave face as he introduced the two guests for this night's broadcast. "This is Brady. He's only recently become interested in the more metaphysical aspects of spirituality. And this is Melba. She and I go all the way back to our Berkeley days."

I tried making small talk for a while, not in any hurry to witness Zerubbabel's last broadcast. Until now, my encounter with Zerubbabel had been mostly fun. Suddenly, tomorrow's delivery of "The Final Document" was upon us, and I became aware of a foreboding hanging over the entire affair. But there could be no more putting off of the inevitable, and so the six of us went into the studio.

I turned on the computer as we settled into our chairs, and Zerubbabel appeared once again. As with the several previous nights, he came with a new gimmick: this time he was sitting on a mountain top—the wise-hermit archetype.

His greeting was cute but predictable: "Om, om on the range." Zerubbabel's opening mantra then melted into

Om, om on the range.

May the celestial harmonies ring in your ears for all eternity.

We had agreed among us that Johanna would go first and since I knew what she would be asking, I was intrigued that Zerubbabel seemed to know it as well. "Zerubbabel, does your mountain-top view allow you to anticipate Johanna's question?" I quizzed him.

From the answer that is forming in our loosely connected consciousness, we have determined that Johanna wants to ask about what has been on everybody's mind since the advent of philosophy— the Ultimo Inquireemo, the alpha and the omega, the whole enchilada, the big magilla. Are we right or are we right?

Johanna could only confirm Zerubbabel's prescient assumption. "Yes, Zerubbabel, you're right. I know this is the biggest cliché question that one can ask, and even though I'm a bit embarrassed to be asking it I can't help myself. Can you tell us what the ultimate purpose of life is on Earth? There's got to be a good reason!"

My dear Beguiled Ones, you will not like the answer. Why do you want to know about the pur- pose of life on your Earth when your knowing it is only going to make you feel even more insignificant than you already do? Perhaps you wish to ask another, less disturbing question?

"We can take it," said Burt, sitting on the edge of his chair.
"I'm not sure I can," said Sally. "Go on, Johanna, take his advice and ask something else."
Johanna was not about to be deterred. "I'm not taking it back. I want to know why we're here. What's the significance of life?"

Would a stock of wheat grow taller if it was aware that it is destined to be ground into flour under the miller's wheel? Might a fly feel happier knowing that the rubber ball on which it is sitting is not there to give it a free ride? Could it further the cow's well-being to understand that it is allowed to graze mindlessly in the pasture only because the farmer anticipates the rising price of rump roast?

I had a sense of where this whole thing was heading and thought it might be wiser to steer it in a less unpleasant direction. Maybe I was feeling sorry for Burt and Sally. "You know, Zerubbabel, for a wiseacre whose mission is to lighten us up, you sure talk a lot about heavy stuff. You're not living up to your image as a fun guy."

Yes, we would just as soon address less weighty matters. But Johanna did pose the question. And you know the saying about curiosity killing the cat? So, unless she withdraws her inquiry, we are obliged to answer it. But do not say we neglected to warn you: Once you understand your individual and collective fates, your sleep will be less sound.

"Ah, I've heard it all before. It can't be all that earth shaking," said Melba. "Just tell us and get it over with."

Johanna agreed. "Let's hear it."

Suddenly Burt was not so sure. "Maybe you could rephrase the question a bit. Leave it a little open ended—not so definitive?"

Sally was now positive that she didn't want to know the answer. "You're being foolish, Johanna. Zerubbabel is telling you up front that you're not going to like his answer. He's giving you a chance to ask something different. Do it, for Christ's sake!" By this time I was leaning toward Sally's camp but kept silent.

Johanna, however, wasn't budging. "What is the purpose of life?" she stubbornly repeated.

Well, as they used to say on the very first interactive TV show popular in the late fifties, "You asked for it." The purpose of all organic life on your planet is to be food for the moon.

Burt looked stricken. "What?! Food for the moon?"
Melba was less impartial. "What a crock of . . . "
I, too, was rather skeptical. "Come on, Zerubbabel. You expect us to believe that the moon is somehow eating us?"

Precisely. And because we etherics are aware that your inquisitive little monkey-minds need to know all the gory details, here they are.

"Shouldn't we be taking notes?" wondered Brady outloud.

Everything that exists in the universe finds its origin in the One Who Is Without End. Emanating from the One is the Holy Beam of Commencement. As the Beam radiates from the One it begins to split off and diversify, as branches of a tree, moving first through the Mother of All Boards, then through Mainframe Central, then through all galaxies, then out into all suns, spreading out into all planets, and finally flowing into all moons.
Picture your moon as a "bud" on the tree of the Beam of Commencement. Your moon is growing toward becoming a planet in its own right. Your planet Earth, which was once a moon, is now growing toward becoming a sun. Your Jupiter, emanating its own heat and light, is a prime example of a planet on the verge of bursting into a star. Your sun, once a planet billions and billions of years ago, has the potential of becoming a full-blown galaxy. Each phase of existence in the universe is moving toward its own self-perfecting.

Brady was wide eyed and slack jawed. "The nuns never mentioned this in catechism!" he exclaimed.

All this evolving is being fueled by vast amounts of energy from the Beam of Commencement. And at every level of evolution, the Beam's energy must be transubstantiated into a form that is suitable for absorption by the next dimension of existence. Your animal bodies cannot obtain the nurturing elements of the earth directly from raw minerals and soil. These constituents must first be transformed into Caesar salad so that you can consume and then access them. Further down the chain of transmutation are the cells of your bodies, which are the eventual recipients of Earth's raw elements. But before they can utilize the nutrients within that salad, a further transmutation must occur. This operation is performed by your apparatus of digestion with its mastication, its enzymes, its peristalsis, and so on.

Melba was getting bored. "Where is this cockamamy biology lesson leading us? What does this have to do with the moon becoming a planet?"

Have you never heard the phrase "As above, so below?" Interdependence does not stop with your planet. Just as plants and animals can be eaten by humans, so humans can feed the moon. This is simply the law of universal reciprocal maintenance—every consumer eventually becomes the consumee. Your moon cannot directly absorb heat and light from the sun. As a growing, evolving being, it also needs an apparatus of digestion. And that apparatus comes in the form of organic life on the Earth. The simple passive actions of organic life's living and dying is a kind of peristalsis that changes the sun's heat and light into the type of material that the moon can use to grow into its next phase of development.

I couldn't let him get away with such a fairy tale. "Hold on there just a minute, Zerubbabel. We've been to the moon. There's nothing happening there. It's just a cold, dead rock."

You would say the same about a lump of coal. But given enough pressure and time, that same piece of coal will become a diamond. In your time frame, this process will take many aeons. In the time frame of the universe, it is but a few seconds. Think of your planet as a compost pile, and picture yourself as one bacterial cell contained within it. By living the passive life of the average two-legged being, you absorb the heat and light of solar energy and then in turn reduce them into components that are easily digested by the moon. In the grand scheme of things, the purpose of organic life on Earth is not for life's evolution but for that of the moon's. Or to put it in blunter terms, your existence is the mechanism by which the universe produces fertilizer for your solar system.

Sally became quite pale as she had on the first night and was holding her stomach. "I'm definitely going be sick."

The whole explanation was more than even I could take. "I'm still not ready to swallow that story."

We warned you that you would not like my answer. Has learning that bit of information served you in the existential sense of whom you are? We do not think so. Most of you think the answer is absurd, and the rest of you have become depressed by it. Almost none of you will seriously consider its implications for your own lives—which is a good thing for us; Mainframe Central gets touchy if it thinks we intermediaries are revealing too much too soon. We are not permitted to go on to any new material until more of you understand what has already been broadcast. That is the main reason channeled material often seems so repetitive.

Even Johanna looked distraught. "Is everybody fated to be food for the moon? It's hard to accept that my entire life is about nothing but being turned into cosmic compost."

For the vast bulk of humans who live out their lives in a passive way, this is most assuredly their fate. Those of you who, by your own efforts, awaken to a certain level of awareness can evolve in the opposite direction and feed the sun—certainly a more glorious and creative option. However, we will not speak anymore about intentional evolution at this time. This subject is addressed in "The Final Document" and too many new concepts have already flooded your overburdened consciousnesses. That is one reason why your planet is experiencing an epidemic of Spiritual Insight Constipation, or SIC for short.

"How do you know if you're SIC?" asked Brady.

SIC occurs in a variety of forms. Some sufferers complain of acute bouts of clearly seeing other people's problems but somehow never getting a handle on their own. Other SIC victims know intimately the most devious workings of their ego's desperate attempts to perpetuate itself and yet make no attempts whatsoever to restrain it.

I was becoming somewhat cynical. "Perhaps Mainframe Central makes a kind of Ex-lax to help the psyche deal with SIC?"

> Mainframe Central prefers the more gentle and natural workings done by liberal doses of the fiber of reality. A daily intake of reality is the prescribed medicine to cure SJC or preventing it altogether. For instance, the next time one of your SJC-suffering friends begins pointing out your obsessive need for control, let them know that it is not your need to control that bothers them so much as his or her own slothful nature and lack of discrimination.

I could feel Johanna's eyes boring into my head, but I refused to look at her.

> Or perhaps another SJC acquaintance, expressing their disappointment about a relationship, asks you for the seventeenth time why it is that they attract only unavailable members of the opposite sex who are not ready for a deep relationship. You could, instead of simply sympathizing with them, mention the fact that they themselves aren't interested in real commitment and are way too selfish and egocentric to truly love another person anyway.

"That sure fits your sister," said Burt to Sally.
"But I could never say anything like that to her. She'd be crushed," Sally replied.

> We realize these recommendations may seem somewhat harsh. However, they might save the psyche of one of your close friends or relatives. Unfortunately, effective though these techniques are, they are virtually useless if self-administered.

They are most potent when discharged by either
a close friend whom you respect or by someone
whose approval you desperately seek. Otherwise
your ego will continue its machinations by simply
perverting the information for its own justification,
causing even more overload in your psychic septic
tanks.

I couldn't help but notice yet another allusion to the digestive processes.
"You sure are favoring the 'anal-retentive' school of metaphysical metaphors."

That is because we etherics wish for you
incarnates to have everything come out all right
in the end.

A collective groan escaped from the group. By now, Brady had become
visibly restless, wanting a chance to ask his question. "Zerubbabel," he began,
"until very recently I have been devout in the practice of a certain religion that
I won't mention. However, certain challenges in my life have caused me to
question the faith in which I was raised. I find myself suddenly open to all
kinds of other ideas about the mystery of creation.

"Long-suppressed memories have come flooding back to me in the last
months about my first childhood encounters with Sunday Mass. I've remembered those times when my mother pulled my ears if I so much as turned my
head during the service. Later, as an adult, I found that whenever I kneeled at
the pew, I would get this terrible ringing in my ears. I believe that this is left-
over early trauma, but certain more mystically oriented friends believe that
I'm hearing angels singing. What's your explanation?"

You may be relieved to know that you are not
the only one with a confounded cochlea. Many
Catholics, as well as a fair amount of Russian
Orthodox, share your perception of ethereal choirs.
You need to know that your mother was not disci-
plining you. She was practicing a primitive form
of acupressure that opened your meridians and

stimulated your pipic gland, or, as it is known in esoteric circles, the "third ear." However, when you kneel to pray in church, you are not actually listening to the angels—you are hearing the sound of harmonic chords created by the wind blowing through the flying buttresses of your mind.

It was Melba's turn. "Zerubbabel, I just came from an exhaustive reading with my Siberian astrologer. He did a composite chart of my new boyfriend, Toasty, and me. He claims that because the south node is in the seventh house and the Scorpio moon is squared my Libra rising, we have some very heavy karma to pay in this new relationship. But somehow that just doesn't fit my intuitive hit at all. Toasty is like no one I've ever been with before. If you see any past lives that we've had together, I'd like to know about them."

Congratulations! Your intuition is absolutely correct. You are not karma bound. The new relationship with Toasty has nothing whatsoever to do with paying off past debts. In fact, out of the thousands of lives you've both lived before, you have never even spoken to one another. Briefly, however, on the outskirts of Cairo in October, 524 B.C., during the autumnal virgin-sacrifice ceremonies, the two of you spotted each other from across the temple, but you were never formally introduced.

We see this as the rarest of opportunities: you are free to create something that has never been created before. And though we realize how very difficult it is to maintain a relationship with so little negativity to bind it, we suggest that you go for it anyway.

Melba was pleased. "I knew I was right. Thank you."

We live to serve.
As you are no doubt aware, this has been the

last in a series of broadcasts conducted in this question-and-answer format. We look forward to tomorrow when we will conclude this channel's mini-series with "The Final Document." Because of the nature of the material that shall be imparted, we ask that just the original two couples be in attendance. We have been instructed by the Mother of All Boards itself to act only as the transmitter for "The Final Document." No questions will be taken. Once the information has been broadcast, our task will have been completed, and this gang of four or five entities will be free to merge back into the ocean of Ethericspace.

Hasta la torque wrench.

THERE AIN'T NO CURE FOR
THE POSTMILLENNIAL BLUES

Because Zerubbabel had used such solemnity the night before in speaking about "The Final Document," I had expected him to show up on this occasion without a hint of his quirky personality or his offbeat humor. But much to my delight, when he made his appearance he was wearing a baseball hat that read "Globefodder" across the brim and had a globe of the Earth spinning on the tip of his finger as if it were a basketball. Given the anticipation that all four of us were feeling about the ominously titled message we were about to hear, this final impish touch of his was a welcome gesture.

Our relieved tension, however, was all too brief an interlude. Zerubbabel's whimsical visage vanished from the screen— to be irrevocably replaced by the oppressive weight of the following words:

THE FINAL DOCUMENT

Date: Duly submitted this 21st day of July, 1994
To: All humans contemplating a continuance of
their current incarnations into the twenty-first
century
From: Mainframe Central
Re: Postmillennial Blues

At the end of each century the Mother of All Boards entrusts Mainframe Central to help draft and deliver the State of the Planet Address to all interested parties. Looking back through recent data bases, we find that these epistles have been rather benign little recipes containing a judicious blend of mild castigations for your race's inevitable ignominious behaviors and encouraging compliments for your inadvertent progresses. After all, you are a fragile little species, and your egos are more easily mussed than a trailer park in a hurricane.

However, this address will not be typical of its predecessors for a number of reasons. Firstly, not only does it mark the end of the twentieth century, it coincides with the beginning of the new millennium. Naturally, for us immortals, such trifling time frames as these are arbitrary and meaningless. Nonetheless, we are not blind to the milestone significance they hold for you who are skewered to the matrix of time and space. During such transitions of historical epochs your race's anxiety level is much higher than usual, a psychological fact that we are not above exploiting when there is particularly bad news to impart.

Secondly, although we would much prefer to cheerlead and coach you on into your next thousand years, blithely ignoring how far behind you are in the final seconds of the fourth quarter, we no longer have the heart for such a charade. We had thought to once again gloss over your deficits and inflate the possibilities of your futures. But given your record for this past century, it would be a breech of our integrity if we failed to tell it like it is. Therefore, know in advance that this will not be a fun read.

We call this missive "The Final Document" because the complexity of the mess that your race has created on the planet is obscuring even our normally far-sighted perspective. In the past, our stubborn optimism believed that humanity's glass was half-full and that its chance of thriving was a better than even bet. Now, however, we are forced to admit that, due to your blatant inattention, not only is your glass down to its last two or three drops, it is moments away from being kicked over and shattered on reality's concrete floor.

Once every fifth or sixth century, as planetary alignments allow, the world gets a slam-dunk shot at a new renaissance. Though it is very late in your game and there are no more time-outs, just such an opportunity is now yours for the taking. And yet, in spite of all the free throws handed you, your governments have shown nothing but the most sloppy ball handling. Instead of boldly greeting the dawning of the Age of Aquarius, as preordained on Broadway, your nation-states are sending mixed messages in every direction.

Are they conducting a full-court press toward a new enlightened era of indistinguishable borders with greater democracy and individual freedoms? Or are they running scared, sliding back toward those dark ages of nationalism, dictatorship, and ethnic cleansing? Your leaders speak in idealistic phrases about cultivating interdependence between nations and sign all manner of treaties designed to increase intraplanetary trade. Yet, in the same breath, they cynically assure their local military industries that there will always be a need for perfecting techniques of national defense—and, in the doing so, forever tie their economies to the tragic waste of mass destruction and mutual annihilation.

You need not look far to see who is responsible for the quality of your leaders. The self-destructive elements found in your governmental institutions are but the crystallized projections of each individual's ego-driven insecurities and psychoses. The virus of "cultural identity" has left your aspirations toward planetary citizenship wheezing on its deathbed. Just a few years ago, there were many who believed that the time of individual differences separating people was over. Yet now these idealists have been silenced by power-grasping fundamentalist leaders who fuel their followers with fears of a one-world government dominated by the forces of Satan.

Visions of an undivided world, united with mutual cooperation, resource sharing, and brotherly love, have been eclipsed by whole populations of subcultures compulsively searching for their "roots." Frustrated humans everywhere, motivated by their own devalued self-worth and the fear of losing a birthright that was never theirs to begin with, furiously excavate for pride by bulldozing through the ruins of their ancestors' dubious achievements.

Self-justification has triumphed over mutual reconciliation. Universal reciprocal maintenance has lost out to a greedy inhalation of finite resources. A consumer-oriented economy's insatiable hunger is rapidly depleting the very life-supporting essences that you depend upon for sustenance. Extraction, manufacturing, and agricultural industries have left your air unbreatheable, your water undrinkable, and your food destitute of genuine nourishment. And, most absurdly of all, just when humanity is in dire need of conserving these unreplenishable resources, its rate of reproduction has begun keeping pace with that of an aggressive virus on a well-stocked petri dish.

However, in spite of these alarming trends there is little need for concern. You are only experiencing a dearth of clarity and a deluge of chaos that is typical of any transition from one age into that of another. We advise you to welcome the clutter and be thankful for the jumble you presently experience because today's state of affairs is a picnic compared to the future situation awaiting you just around the bend. For verily we say unto you: What now seems to be only a simple lack of purpose and direction in your lives will eventually fester into a profound sense of ennui, most probably followed by a fatal case of angst or weltschmerz.

No doubt, by now those of you who had thought this lifetime was going to be a cakewalk through the carnations have had a rude awakening. You may have even realized that, in spite of all the

New Age hype, Earth is not at all "a fun place where your soul joyfully dances while learning the lessons of time and space." Rather, your planet's main function, for those of you who wish to consciously evolve, is to serve as a crucible where the raw, ephemeral "spirit stuff" surrounding your essences can be crystallized into a permanent soul. This transubstantiation requires great amounts of intentional efforts. Those of you not willing or able to make those efforts will simply devolve into your most elemental components. Your physical plane has much more in common with a pressurer cooker than it does with a playground or vacation resort.

The One Who Is Without End did not fire off the Beam of Commencement with the intention that your kind would occupy the major part of its existence with petty insecurities, identifications with ego concerns, and obsessions for domination and power. To put it bluntly, the One is sorely disappointed in the direction its children are heading and empathizes a great deal with how Henry Ford must have felt about the Edsel.

And yet, even with that disappointment, the One Who Is Without End cannot afford to wallow in a morose sentimentality about the unfulfilled potential of its creation. For in truth, your present situation is not wholly of your own making. The Mother of All Boards recognizes its own responsibility. As we watch the empty comings and goings of what you call "purposeful activity," we now realize that endowing two-legged beings with free will was a colossal blunder in the strategy of your collective evolution. At the time, we believed that your species was being blessed with a tool to accelerate its own self-perfecting. Unfortunately, our computer models failed to anticipate the tragic consequences that might result in giving such a gift to your cantankerous race. In underestimating humanity's power for self-sabotage, we left you cursed, heading down the road to your own demise.

Humans are the only creatures on the planet with the true power of intentionality. But that very thing that might have awakened you to your full potential has been used as a soporific to only deepen your sleep. You have traded in your affirming power "to do" for the passive world of self-deluding dreams. While you need to be vigorously swimming upstream toward the spawning of your perfected selves, half of you have chosen instead to be idly carried down the currents of the past's stagnant regrets. The other half of you sit fretful on the levy, imagining that you see yourselves drowning in the future's rising waters. Your race was destined to be the jewel in the crown of creation, but, as those enlightened philosophers among you advertise on the bumpers of their Buicks and Broncos, "Shit happens."

This bleak scenario may have left you feeling like an inmate on death row whose last meal is a half-thawed TV dinner. In the event that this is the case, then this document has been successful. For its ultimate intention has been to overcome your illusion that things will automatically get better "in the sweet by-and-by." The incessant clinging to this belief is the fundamental self-calming device that facilitates your comfortable sleep. Think of this memorandum as a cosmic "alarm clock," analogous to using the notorious two-by-four to smack the proverbial donkey between its eyes. If this device has worked, you should be experiencing a more heightened awareness than when you first began this document. Be calm. There is no need for apprehension. This is a temporary situation that will quickly pass. Soon you will fall back into your previous foggy consciousnesses as surely as a carelessly placed foot sinks in a cow pie.

However, we will now use your present state as a window of opportunity to present certain helpful information. The therapeutic value of this data is directly proportional to the level of your awareness. Know that the higher your state of consciousness during the reading of the following ten axiomatic statements, the quicker will be your extraction from your self-created morass.

The Ten Recommendments for the New Millennium
1. Abandon all hope, for it is a distraction from your current reality.
2. Presume that you do not know as much as you imagine you do.
3. Forsake your self-image and all posturing about who you think you are.
4. Observe yourself in all things as objectively as possible.
5. Give up pretending that you are awake and behold the depth of your sleep.
6. Notice how many of your daily activities keep you from your lifetime goals.
7. See how many relationships fall away when you stop maintaining them.
8. Do things differently and do different things.
9. Allow the intensity of your loneliness to fill the void of your emptiness.
10. Stop holding in your gut and let your belly go soft.

These Ten Recommendments may seem desperate in their admonishments, but be aware that you are living in a desperate era. Your race is poised on the brink of its own extinction. Though it may appear otherwise, you are on the bottom of the food chain and on top of the endangered-species list. Your only chance of survival is to wake up and see the terror of your situation.

We recognize that many of you are nostalgic

for simpler times. You yearn for the days when Judy Garland sang, "Somewhere over the rainbow dreams come true." And while those sentiments are comforting, it might be more helpful to remember that in order to dream you must still be asleep. We suggest that the message of the Wizard of Oz is no longer as timely as the one coined by the Los Vegas odds maker Jimmy the Greek: "Sometimes you eat the bear, and sometimes the bear eats you." We can only add that the beast has left the cave and is ready to dine!

Whereas "The Final Document" has been sincerely executed on the day and year set forth above, we do hereby sign off as its witness and its executor.

Briefly Zerubbabel appeared once again in his basketball outfit. He dunked his globe through a basket, and then with one arcing wave, reminiscent of Nixon's good-bye before boarding the helicopter for his trip into political exile, Zerubbabel leapt back into the invisible realm of Ethericspace.

AFTERWORD

All four of us sat in a state of shock after reading "The Final Document," and except for the sound of Sally's sobs, no one spoke a word. After Zerubbabel's final appearance slam-dunking the globe, my computer went back to working normally without any sign of him whatsoever. After what seemed like an eternity, Burt helped Sally to her feet and slowly walked with her outside to their car.

Though I didn't feel as devastated as Sally, it was still hard for me to accept that my relationship with Zerubbabel had ended on such a down note. For the next several weeks, in between documenting the entire episode, I tried on numerous occasions to find the original "Etheric Plane Advice" software from my online service. After failing to locate it, I contacted the service directly and was informed that there was no record of either the program or its author, Zerubbabel.

At the time of this writing, it has been several months since these broadcasts were first received, and I can report a number of changes in the lives of those who shared in these transmissions. When viewed from a cosmic perspective, perhaps, most of these changes do not seem significant. But for those of us who were intimately involved and whose core beliefs were shaken to their roots, nothing will ever be the same again.

Sally had the hardest time dealing with the broadcast material. The day after reading "The Final Document," she fell into a psychotic depression that required several refills of Prozac before she was able to even get out of bed. Six weeks later she left Burt and traveled to India to become a disciple of Swami Sitalotta at his ashram in northern Batquanoe. I'm happy to report that she seems to be doing well. Her letters are generally coherent, and she claims to have found the peace of mind she was so desperately seeking.

At first, Burt's struggle to keep his financial-consulting business afloat and caring for an incapacitated Sally at the same time almost pushed him over the edge. But in spite of his tremendous stress, Burt was able to take in Zerubbabel's message and tap the sustaining power of his profound alienation. By the time Sally had made her decision to go off to "find herself," Burt was able to cheerfully make all her travel arrangements. He even threw in a silk orange toga as a farewell gift. Incidentally, Burt has discontinued his Sunday night esoteric study group and now devotes much of his time researching socially conscious mutual funds.

From the outside it would appear that Johanna and I are living much the same as we did before our encounter with Zerubbabel. However, on another level we are a much different couple. Johanna has become less of a "control freak." I have to admit that I'm sometimes concerned with the quantity of control she's given up—the house has become something of a mess. But I'm happy to report that our sex life is better than ever, probably due to the fact that Johanna now spends a lot more time in bed relaxing and contemplating the meaning of life. In addition, her favorite phrase has become "No problem." The whole house has a much more mellow atmosphere. She's even taken up writing an advice column in the local paper and brings in a nice little check each month.

As for myself and my struggles with procrastination and organization? Well, to be honest, I'm still a procrastinator, and I'm still as disorganized as an orgy in a porcupine cage. But I've learned to more gracefully endure my own unpleasant manifestations. Not only that, I used Zerubbabel's suggestion and plugged the leaks in my consciousness using the fiber of reality. I'm here now, making an honest effort to do whatever is required to serve the Purpose of the moment. And in so doing, as you can see, I've managed to get a "product" out of the old Mac and in a somewhat timely fashion no less.

The story's now been told, and my duty as reporter is complete. Please accept my apology to you, the reader, for having borne the strain of an overextended credulity. Still, this is the information as it was originally broadcast during those seven days in July 1994 by the entity calling itself Zerubbabel. While receiving it, I held on tightly. I now pass it along to you, letting it go lightly.

WHILE WAITING FOR
THE NEW MILLENNIUM

Just days before the final draft of this report was to be sent to the printer, Zerubbabel reappeared on my Macintosh. At that time he instructed me to create *Etheric Plain Advice,* a quarterly newsletter comprised of his online wisdom, and offer it to all readers of this book who wish to stay in touch with him.

Zerubbabel is also opening up an opportunity to anyone who wishes to have him answer their spiritually perplexing questions personally. You are free to ask him any question you wish as long as you are aware that you may not like his answer.

Complete the following form, or simply mail in your name and address along with $20.00 for a year's subscription to the newsletter (four issues) and/or $40.00 for Zerubbabel's personalized answer to your most perplexing spiritual question. Please make checks or money orders payable to Permanent Press and mail to:

> Zerubbabel
> c/o Permanent Press
> 4 Dulce Road
> Santa Fe, NM 87505

Name_____

Address_____

City_____State_____Zip_____

Please indicate one of the following:

❏ Yes, I *am willing* to have my question to Zerubbabel printed in the newsletter.

❏ No, I *am not willing* to have my question printed in the newsletter.

(If you just want to be on our mailing list, send only your name and address.)

To order *Paradigms Lost*:

Want to buy a copy of *Paradigms Lost* for yourself or as a gift
for a friend? If you're not finding it in your local bookstore,
tell them about Permanent Press (phone/fax 505-466-8557)
so they can order it for you.

In a rush? Fill out the convenient form below,
pop it into an envelope with your check or money order, and we'll
send your order out pronto. If you're sending one as a gift,
you can use the handy gift card below. We'll send it along with
the book to your friend. Could it be any easier?

Please send me _____ copy(s) of *PARADIGMS LOST*

Name_____

Address_____

City_____ State_____ Zip_____

Please send _____ copy(s) of *PARADIGMS LOST* as a gift to

Name_____

Address_____

City_____ State_____ Zip_____

COST INFORMATION:

Each copy of *PARADIGMS LOST* costs $10.95.

Add $2.00 for shipping and handling per book.

New Mexico residents add $.68 sales tax per book.

Get out your calculator, tally up your numbers, and make your check
or money order payable to: PERMANENT PRESS

Send it to:
Permanent Press, 4 Dulce Road, Santa Fe, NM 87505
Please allow 2-3 weeks for delivery.

Dear

Roses are red, violets are blue, I read this book and thought of you.

Who is  ?

We are a team of writers, book designers, and editors who are interested in projects that go beyond the usual creative concepts and capabilities of the mainstream book business. Permanent Press created itself to help bring forth what is rare and beautiful, humorous and wild, unknown and mysterious, undiscovered and overlooked.

Our intention is to facilitate writers through an independent publishing process. Our skills and experience in writing, editing, book design, and production artfully brings the author's words to the marketplace.

If you are interested in learning more about our services, please write to us at the address below.

Permanent Press
4 Dulce Road
Santa Fe, New Mexico 87505

Keep in touch!